GW00577991

A RICHLY YIELDING PIECE OF GROUND

A HISTORY OF FOWEY CONSOLS MINE 1813 TO 1867

by

J. B. Lewis

"I have been twice about Wheal Treasure since I saw
you and the workmen appear in good heart. Let us make
a mine of her and she'll make us many friends."

J. T. Austen to Adam Thomson. 3rd May 1817.

CORNISH HILLSIDE PUBLICATIONS

St Austell, Cornwall

First published 1997 by
CORNISH HILLSIDE PUBLICATIONS
St Austell, Cornwall PL25 4DW

© J. B. Lewis 1997

ISBN 1900147 05 X paperback
ISBN 1900147 06 8 clothbound

Cover by The Design Field, Truro.
Bust of J.T. (Austen) Treffry on cover and page 104
photographed by Roger Dovey, St. Austell.
Location maps drawn by Roger Penhallurick, Truro.
Printed and bound by Short Run Press Ltd, Exeter EX2 7LW.

CONTENTS

Errata

p. 99 Line 18 24" should be, 24″.

    Line 20 18" should be, 18″.

p. 112 Line 6 18,104 should be, £18,104.

p. 153 Fig. 2. The Downward Stroke, final paragraph;

    Line 1 The Water pressure engine's should be, The Water pressure engines.

FOREWORD

All of us who are interested in the mining and industrial history of Cornwall should welcome this fascinating history of Fowey Consols. Too little has been written about the mines of mid-Cornwall which contributed much to the prosperity of the central part of the county in the first half of the nineteenth century. Fowey Consols, with its great engine-house dominating the landscape, is thought at one time to have supported a population of over seven thousand largely in the Tywardreath, St. Blazey and Luxulyan area.

The driving force in creating Fowey Consols was the outstanding entrepreneur and venture capitalist Joseph Thomas Treffry. He inherited a half-share of an ancient but run-down landed estate and bought out the other part-owners. On this small capital base he built a huge industrial empire encompassing mines, quarries, ports, shipping and railways. When he died in 1850 he was said to be the largest employer of labour in the West of England.

Joseph Thomas Treffry never married and devoted his life to his work. He was ascetic, self-disciplined and forceful with astonishing drive and energy. He was a fair but demanding employer who inspired respect and admiration from his work people.

All were impressed by his sense of vision and by his ability and dedication. His first appointments were at six o'clock in the morning and he was reported to have answered all his business correspondence on the day it was received. It is recorded that he never took a holiday and rarely spent a night away from Fowey even when his historic family mansion, Place, was being re-built. In this imaginative re-building he encouraged young Cornish craftsmen such as Neville Northy Burnard of Altarnun, the sculptor who worked at Place as a young man and Robert Whale the artist also of Altarnun who undertook some fine decorative work at Place. It is appropriate that Burnard's marble bust of Joseph Thomas Treffry should grace the front cover of this book and that Robert Whale's fine painting of the Treffry Viaduct should form part of the back cover.

We must indeed be grateful to Jim Lewis for producing such an interesting and scholarly book about Fowey Consols and its remarkable creator.

DAVID TREFFRY, Place, Fowey. August 1996.

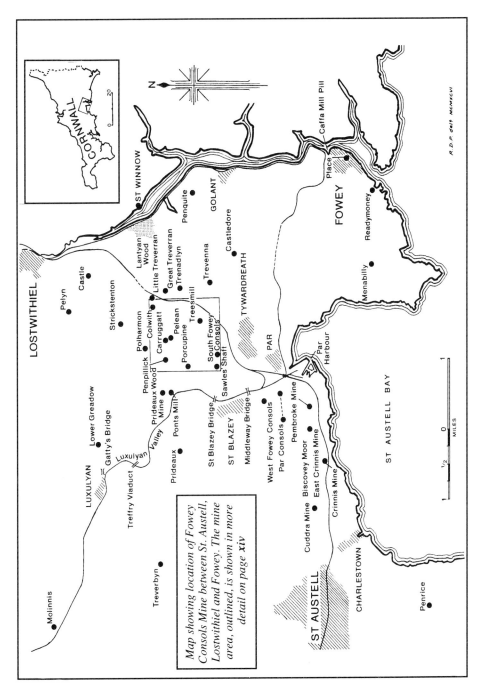

Map showing location of Fowey Consols Mine between St. Austell, Lostwithiel and Fowey. The mine area, outlined, is shown in more detail on page xiv

v

INTRODUCTION

The Mining Journal of 19th February 1881 published a letter from a correspondent describing Fowey Consols mine as "a richly yielding piece of ground". The description was well warranted. The mine operated in the period from 1813 to 1867 and during this time it produced 383,000 tons of copper ore which sold for £2.2 million approximately. At its height in the 1830s and early 1840s it employed more than 1,700 people. Towards the end of its life in 1860 it was estimated that the sett covered 1,500 acres with 7 miles of shafts and 150 miles of levels underground, with a maximum depth from surface at Bottrall's shaft of about 2,000 feet.

The site of the mine lies approximately 3½ miles north west of Fowey and one mile north east of St. Blazey in south Cornwall. The northern section is situated near the top of Penpillick Hill and the remainder of the sett slopes predominantly south towards Par and Tywardreath. The reason why the mine took its name from Fowey and not from nearer towns and villages is due to the man who overshadowed its history.

Joseph Thomas Austen was baptised in Plymouth on 1st May 1782 and acquired the Treffry estates and the mansion of Place in Fowey through his mother who was born Susan Ann Treffry. He initially bought shares in the mine at a time when he was endeavouring to promote the trade of Fowey and when he was also deeply involved in the local politics of this rotten borough. With its winners and losers the complex early history of Fowey Consols could have served as a plot for a Dickens novel. Austen obtained control and soon after found himself the virtual owner of one of the biggest mines that Cornwall ever saw. His forceful character and great energy drove the mine through a turbulent period of great social upheaval, ruffling some feathers along the way. He took the family name of Treffry in February 1838 when the mine was at its peak, and when he died in 1850 the mine was in decline.

Virtually everyone interested in the mining history of Cornwall knows something about Fowey Consols, and it is hoped that this book will add more to what is generally known about the mine as well as being of interest to the general reader. For those unfamiliar with copper mining in Cornwall a brief preface follows, and some further notes appear in the glossary.

Most of the early information in this book is culled from the Treffry, Rashleigh and Harvey papers at the Cornwall Record Office and it has been selectively referenced in the text. On a few occasions the English in some of the quotations used has been slightly modernised.

The following abbreviations have been used in the 'Notes' for each chapter:

CRO   Cornwall Records Office
MJ   Mining Journal
RCG   Royal Cornwall Gazette
WB   West Briton

ACKNOWLEDGMENTS

I would like to thank everyone who has assisted me and so freely shared their information on Fowey Consols, in particular Ken Brown, Justin Brooke, Maurice Cooke (great grandson of William West), the late Ron Fitzmaurice, Courtenay Smale, Roger Penhallurick, Isabel Pickering and the archivists of the Royal Archives and Lloyds Bank. My thanks are also due to Miss Angela Broome of the Royal Institution of Cornwall, Mrs. Christine North of the Cornwall Records Office (copyright reserved) and Terry Knight of the Cornish Studies Library at Redruth and their colleagues who have been enormously helpful in providing me with most of the research material used in this book. Tony Brooks, David Treffry, Derek Reynolds & Justin Brooke have been kind enough to read the final draft and make helpful suggestions. I would like to thank Liz, my wife, for carrying out much of the research and for her tolerance and Charles Thurlow for his comments and encouragement.

PREFACE

Copper ore deposits occur in veins or lodes where they were deposited in fissures in the earth's crust millions of years ago along with other metallic and non-metallic minerals. Lodes are often irregular in size and mineral content. Searching underground for economic deposits of ore could be a long, expensive and often unsuccessful business with a fortunate few making vast fortunes from the mining industry.

To reach and open up ore deposits (development work) it was necessary to sink shafts and drive tunnels (levels) through solid rock. Holes were drilled in the rock using a metal rod with one end having a sharpened, chisel shaped steel bit. One man usually held this borer in place, slowly rotating it in the hole while two colleagues beat the opposite end of the rod with sledge hammers to apply the power to drill the holes. The holes were then charged with gunpowder and fired, a hazardous operation with crude fuzes prior to the invention of the miner's safety fuze in Cornwall in 1831. When ore deposits were found they were removed (stoping), again by using gunpowder, and the ore bearing veinstone was hauled to the surface using horse, water or steam power. Waste rock also had to be hauled to the surface for disposal unless it could be dumped back in old abandoned workings underground. Once at surface (at grass) the ore bearing rock was processed to sort the ore from the waste as far as practicable. This processed ore was then examined and sampled at the mine by representatives of the smelting companies (samplers). The various parcels of ore were usually kept on the mine until they were sold at ticketings which were generally held weekly, normally at Redruth or Truro. Based on what their samplers had found the smelting companies made sealed bids for the ores for sale at the ticketing, the highest bidder being successful. The recovery of copper metal from its ores required large amounts of coal and the ore was then transported by sea to Swansea in South Wales for smelting. The metal content of the copper ore was from 6% to 9%.

Hand in hand with the growth in copper mining came the need to improve the methods of pumping water from the mines as they became deeper. Water was a huge asset at surface where it was needed to help dress (process) the copper ore and power machinery, and a disadvantage underground where it had to be removed to allow mining to take place. Steam engines were eventually installed on all deep mines to drain them, the cylinder size of the engine determining its power. The cost of buying and transporting coal for fuel from South Wales was considerable, and much effort was made by Cornish engineers in bringing the Cornish beam pumping engine to a very high state of fuel efficiency. At Fowey Consols water wheels and water pressure engines provided most of the power needed.

LIST OF ILLUSTRATIONS

GLOSSARY

Adit. A level driven to drain a mine, often started at the foot of a hill.

Adventurer. Shareholder in a mining company before limited liability [1857], in law a partner sharing losses and profits.

Bal maiden. Woman or girl employed at surface on a mine.

Borer. A steel rod with a cutting edge for drilling holes for gunpowder. Often held by one man while two others beat it with sledge hammers.

Burrow. Heap of waste rock raised from a mine, often around a shaft.

Call. Amount per share to be paid by adventurers to cover a mine's costs.

Captain. Manager or assistant manager of a mine.

Coarse work. Poor quality ore. (?)

Core. A working shift, normally eight hours but sometimes only six.

Costean(ing) pits. Prospecting pits sunk in search of lodes.

Crosscut. A level driven at an angle to a lode.

Development. Unproductive work underground to reach and open up a mineral deposit.

Double-acting. A steam-engine with both strokes of the piston powered.

Dry. Changing-house for miners.

Dues or Dish. The fraction of the ore or proceeds of sale of ore received by the mineral lord, in consideration of his granting a sett.

Fathom. 6 feet or 1.8288 metres, the traditional unit of measurement in Cornish mines.

Flat Rods. Horizontal rods transmitting power from a water wheel or steam engine to pumps at a distant shaft.

Footway shaft. A shaft with ladders in it.

Fork (in fork). Drained.

Grass (at grass). At surface.

Halvans. Refuse from prime copper ore needing further dressing to make it merchantable.

Kibble. Iron bucket for raising ore, waste rock or water from a mine.

Killas. Sedimentary rock.

Kindly. Favourable for mineral.

Launder. An open wooden trough to carry water or slimes by gravity.

Leader. The rich part of a lode. A branch or string of ore which leads to a lode.

Leat. A man-made water-course.

Level. A horizontal passage in a mine.

Lord of the soil/Mineral Lord. Owner of the minerals in a piece of ground.

Overshot. A water wheel powered by water flowing over the top, the usual type on mines.

Pare. A gang of two or more men.

Pitch. A working place underground, usually where tributers or tutworkers were employed.

Pitman. Man who services and superintends the pumps in a mine.

Pitwork. Pumping machinery and associated devices.

Plat. A platform, usually for loading or unloading.

Rise or raise. Connection driven upwards between levels in a mine, not reaching surface.

Rotten borough. Before 1832, a borough able to elect one or more MPs, though having very few voters.

Sample. To take a small part of a parcel of ore for assaying; the amount so taken.

Saving work. Ore worth dressing to make it merchantable.

Sett. A lease to work mining ground; the piece of ground leased for mining.

Setting day. The day on which tribute and tutwork pitches were bid for.

Sheers. Sheerlegs, or long pieces of timber in the form of an inverted 'V' placed over a shaft, for lowering pumps and timber into a mine.

Spale. A fine for the non-completion of a task.

Stamps. A mill for pulverising poorer quality copper ores. They consisted of a row of vertical wooden rods called lifters, with iron stamp heads on the ends. A horizontal barrel revolved behind the lifters, the teeth on the barrel raising each lifter in turn and letting it drop by its own weight on the ore being crushed.

Standard. The value placed on a ton of copper metal in ore, i.e. the value of a quantity of copper ore sufficient to produce one ton of copper metal including an amount called returning charges which covered the smelters' expenses such as transport costs, fuel and labour. The returning charge was normally £2.15.0. per ton. The use of the standard is an approximate way of comparing copper prices over a period of time. It is not always a true market indicator. For further details see 'Interpreting the Cornish Copper Standard' by Edmund Newell in the Journal of the Trevithick Society, Vol. 13 (1986).

Stem. See 'Core'.

Sturt. A very profitable contract for a tributer, arising when a rich pocket of ore was found in an otherwise poor pitch.

Sump men. Pitmens' assistants; shaft sinkers.

Ticketing. Weekly sales of copper ore by sealed tender or ticket.

Tribute. Tributers' share of ore or sale proceeds of ore, expressed as so much in the £.

Tributers. Self-employed miners whose pay is a certain proportion of the value of the ore they raise.

Tutwork. Work done at a fixed price per fathom.

Wheal. The Cornish for work, hence a mine working; a common element in mine names.

Whim. Device for raising ore, waste and water out of a mine, driven by water wheels, horses or steam engines.

Winze. A vertical shaft between levels which does not reach to surface.

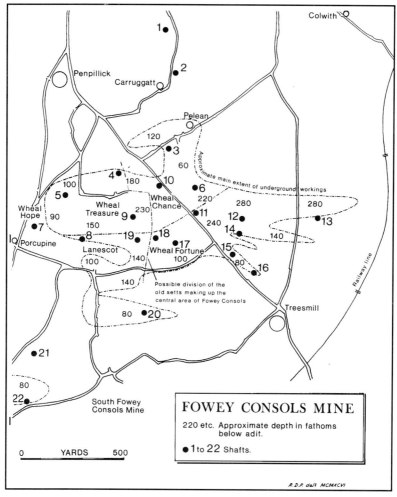

Map showing shafts and setts.
The main Fowey Consols shafts are shown above. To simplify the central area of
the mine the following shafts shown on the de la Beche map on page 63
have been omitted: Coates's, Powne's, Remfry's, Tremayne's.

Numbered shafts:	5. Anthony's	11. Pidler's*	17. Ray's
1. Kendall's North	6. West's	12. Bottrall's	18. Thomson's
2. Carruggatt	7. Tregaske's	13. Henrietta's	19. Sampson's
3. John's	8. Kendall's	14. Blues	20. Hodge's
4. Austen's	9. Union	15. Polsue's	21. Seymour's
	10. Trathan's	16. Mundic	22. Sawle's

*Man engine

CHAPTER I

DEBT AND DISCORD

FOWEY CONSOLS mine was a consolidation or amalgamation of five separate mining ventures near St. Blazey. Wheal Treasure, Wheal Fortune and Wheal Chance began to work in 1813 and they became the original Fowey Consolidated Mines in 1822. The mine was generally known as Fowey Consols from the outset. Wheal Hope was subsequently taken in sometime after 1830, probably at the same time that Lanescot mine became part of the final consolidation in 1836. Wheal Treasure, Wheal Fortune and Wheal Chance bordered one another, with Wheal Hope lying a little way to the west near the St. Blazey to Lostwithiel road. Wheal Treasure was the most productive mine and was followed in importance by Wheal Fortune. Wheal Chance seems to have raised very little ore in its early days although major discoveries were made there in later years.[1] Wheal Hope probably started operations at the same time as the other mines but never produced ore in significant quantities throughout its existence. These mines were initially worked separately but the mainly local adventurers (shareholders) had a substantial common share ownership in each. Lanescot mine lay to the south of Wheal Treasure and was opened about 1817, operating as an independent concern until 1836.

In the early years of the nineteenth century many Cornishmen believed that there was little worth mining east of Truro Bridge. The initially unsuccessful Crinnis copper mine was situated on the coast of St. Austell Bay some three miles to the south west of the future Fowey Consols and it was described as "not worth a pipe of baccy (tobacco)" by a Captain Joseph Mitchell in 1808.[2] This sett was taken up by Joshua Rowe of Torpoint in 1809 and proved to be very profitable. In 1811 it produced 2,136 tons of copper ore and 6,304 tons in the following year, increasing rapidly to 10,108 tons in 1813 and 10,551 tons in 1814.[3] This ore was found less than 50 fathoms from surface, and it seems likely that its spectacular success would have encouraged potential mining investors to look for favourable ground in the neighbourhood of St. Blazey and Tywardreath. How the Fowey Consols lodes were discovered on the hill running north from the Lanescot hamlet to Penpillick is not recorded, but in the 1820s and 1830s costeaning pits were regularly used to search for lodes in the properties adjoining the mine, and it is probable that the lodes in the mine itself were discovered using this method. These were pits dug through the soil down to bedrock to find promising mineral veins which outcropped at the surface. Clearly some indications of worthwhile copper deposits were found, and within one year of the commencement of Wheal Treasure, Wheal Fortune and Wheal Chance J. T. Austen of Fowey purchased a 1/64th share in each mine in 1814.[4]

Production at the mines started slowly, and in an advertisement for the sale of shares in Wheal Treasure dated 9th. June 1815 there were said to be 80 tons of ore at surface and by October the adventurers were advertising for a second hand steam pumping engine to help drain the mine. The advertisement stated that it was to be "complete, on Boulton and Watt's plan, from 36 to 40 inch cylinder (Double)."[5] This would have been an engine of medium power, the word double indicating that both strokes of the piston were steam powered. In December 1815 a "Notice to Creditors" was placed in the Royal Cornwall Gazette, possibly indicating a significant reorganization amongst the adventurers. Apart from Austen other noteworthy shareholders were a wealthy clergyman, the Rev. Robert Walker of St. Winnow, a member of the landed gentry, John Colman Rashleigh of Prideaux and also a John Vivian. It is a strong possibility that he was the John Vivian who, together with his brother Joseph, had been granted the sett of Crinnis mine in 1794.[6] Both men were miners, and having apparently allowed the sett to lapse they subsequently had the chastening experience of watching Joshua Rowe find success there. If this was the case, then having seen a fortune slip through their fingers once, either by bad luck or by a combination of a lack of effort and/or investment, it was to be expected that John Vivian would not have wished to make the same mistake twice. A steam pumping engine for Wheal Treasure was obtained from a Mr. Fox,[7] and by June 1816 it was said to be on the verge of being put to work. By now the mine was seriously in debt, and correspondence indicates that if the engine was ever paid for then it was only with some difficulty. It is probable that costly development work was being undertaken, and the very large fall in the copper standard would have adversely affected the projected income of the mine. (The standard figure used by the mines and copper smelters indicated the market value of the quantity of copper ore needed to produce one ton of copper metal including the smelters' expenses, and as such is an approximate way of comparing copper prices over a period of time.) The end of the war against France brought in a national recession, and the standard declined 25% between 1814 and 1816 to an average figure of £98.13.0. The mine temporarily stopped at the end of 1816. Despite this Adam Thomson, a Lostwithiel timber and general merchant, bought a 1/64th share on 30th December 1816. The dealings between Austen and Thomson significantly affected the history of the mines over the next few years. They were both men with comparatively little capital, and they co-operated to obtain the management of Wheal Treasure for themselves. Austen could see the potential there, and on 26th January 1817 he told Thomson "I am sure, as far as in a concern of this sort certainty can be calculated on, that by due economy we may make this mine a good concern."

The two men wished to take over the management of the mine to enable them to promote their interests beyond merely sharing in any profits it made. They wanted to ensure that the shipment of copper ore to South Wales for smelting continued from Austen's wharves in Fowey and to provide Thomson with a favoured position in supplying materials to Wheal Treasure. Thomson had a poor opinion of mining shares as an investment, and the main incentive for him was to become an in-adventurer. If he supplied the mine with goods and if it paid its bills it would be a guaranteed source of profit to him, whether the mine itself was profitable or not.[8] In addition to their joint mining venture Austen and Thomson were also collaborating in the local politics of Fowey. For years Austen had been involved in bitter disputes with the corrupt Corporation which administered the town.[9] The Corporation was empowered under the town's Charter, and in 1817 Thomson was assisting Austen's political faction (the Blues) in opposing the granting of a new Charter.

The principal owners of the land on which the mines were situated were the Kendall family of Pelyn, Lostwithiel and the Tremaynes of Heligan, near St. Austell, together with Edward Pidler or Pedlar of Pelean and a Mr. W. Polsue. The Rev. H. H. Tremayne had wide mining interests in Cornwall, and owned part of the mineral rights to Polgooth mine, which was situated to the west of St. Austell. These mineral lords stood to gain financially by charging a rent based on a fraction of the value of the ores produced (dues) and they were prepared to co-operate in the re-opening of the mine. On 8th February 1817 Austen told Thomson "Mr. Tremayne yesterday consented to abate his dues to 1/10th, which example Mr. Polsue will no doubt follow. We may consider the going to work again of Wheal Treasure as certain." On 1st February Austen had written to Thomson "Your agent may know from Mr. Petherick who will sell shares in the three mines for we must make one concern of them, and I think shares may be bought from £30 to £50 each . . . Mr. Walker is quite in spirits about putting the mine to work again." Thomas Petherick was Austen's chief mining agent and representative, and the consolidation of the mines was clearly an objective from an early stage. The mine was at work by May 1817, and in the summer a meeting was held in Bodmin at which Walker, Colman Rashleigh, Thomson and Austen were present. Austen and Thomson had made their proposals about the future management of Wheal Treasure, and it was decided at the meeting that there would be an equalisation of shareholdings between the four of them and the other adventurers on whose behalf Walker and Colman Rashleigh acted. John Vivian was about to forfeit his share(s) in the mine to repay his business debts, and it could be that the departure of this experienced miner left the gap in its management that Austen and Thomson were very happy to fill. They both had to buy additional shares but Austen could not, or would not, provide the cash himself. The necessary funds were provided by Thomson and the shares were purchased in his name. The fact that Thomson was a partner in the North Cornwall Bank at Bodmin is perhaps an indication of where he found the money, his two other partners in that venture being E. J. Glynn of Glynn, near Bodmin and E. W. W. Pendarves of Camborne.[10] At the meeting it was also seemingly decided that E. J. Glynn should be a part of this adjustment of shareholdings, although he was not made aware of this agreement. Thomson was shortly to hold shares in his name and paid for by him (or the bank) of which a third was said to be his, one third belonged to Austen and the remaining third was the property of Glynn. He entered into this arrangement because Austen assured him that Wheal Treasure would be successful, and that he would guarantee him against any losses arising from their political activities in Fowey.[11]

The captain at Wheal Treasure was John Hitchens of Par, and on his advice Austen bought two additional shares in July 1817. Benjamin Wood, the former manager of Crinnis mine, was fully aware of the opportunities now being provided by the mines, and was also keen to supply them with materials. In August Austen told Thomson "Petherick has just been here to say that B. Wood has offered Hitchens £40 for 4 shares in Wheal Fortune mine. His price is £50 – Wood's view must be for the supply of her as we can hardly calculate now on a majority. Petherick thinks by all means that Wood should be kept out and that we had better give the £50 rather than lose them or have an opponent." By now Wheal Treasure was down to 40 fathoms, and showing the best leader of copper that the mine had seen. On the 19th September Austen sent a Mr. John Cock to bid for him at the Queen's Head Inn at St. Austell, where three 1/64ths. shares in Wheal Treasure were being sold "for the benefit of the mortgage and non-payment of costs." Cock successfully purchased one of these shares for £70, a share belonging to the unfortunate John Vivian. These shares had been mortgaged to E. W. W. Pendarves as security for a loan of £1,500 made to the adventurers of Wheal Treasure. Clearly the proceeds from the sale of the three shares would not have been sufficient to repay all the borrowing and it left a substantial amount still to be repaid. Whilst the financial problem remained at Wheal Treasure opportunities were occuring elsewhere. On the 4th November 1817 Austen wrote to Thomson to say that the "Lanescot adventurers determined yesterday that their ores should come here (Fowey) – don't let anyone step in before you in the timber trade there!" The Lanescot sett had been taken up by adventurers looking for the western extension of the Wheal Fortune lodes, and, as in the other parts of the setts, the ownership of the mineral rights was fragmented. The main mineral lords were again the Kendall and Tremayne families, with J. S. G. Sawle of Penrice owning several fields in the southern part of the Lanescot sett.

For the twelve months ending 30th June 1818 Wheal Treasure produced 1,202 tons of copper ore, and in addition to this record high output the standard had recovered so that the proceeds at £7,413 were only just short of the total income received in the previous three years. Despite this on 17th September Thomson wrote to Austen: "At Wheal Treasure meeting yesterday we came to the resolution of instantly stopping the mine and selling the materials – Messrs. Walker and (Colman) Rashleigh are very willing to carry on Wheal Fortune, and if the dues could be got to a moderate rate I have no doubt but Wheal Treasure can soon be put to work again." Wheal Fortune was, however, the first mine to close and the optimism evident in the letter was to be misplaced. The reason for these difficulties was that the Wheal Treasure adventurers were £4,000 in debt to the North Cornwall Bank and this was probably the major factor in the closure decision, especially if more development work was needed in the mine. The degree of Austen's personal involvement in its management is not known, but the overall situation could be said to be a template for his future industrial activities, the high output of the mine illustrating his great energy and initiative in achieving his goals, and the debt at the bank indicating his willingness to spend large sums of money in pursuit of them. With the two mines in close proximity it is probable that Wheal Fortune was at least partially dependent on Wheal Treasure for both ore dressing and pumping. With the various adventurers having shares in both mines it would have made little sense to duplicate expensive plant and machinery. On 5th December 1818 the following advertisement appeared in the Royal Cornwall Gazette giving an inventory of the equipment on the mine:-

MINE MATERIALS— On Tuesday the 8th Day of December next, and on following days, precisely by ten o'clock in the morning, will be peremptorily sold by auction, at Wheal Treasure Mine, in the Parish of Tywardreath, all the materials of the said mine consisting of:-
1 Steam Engine (Boulton & Watts, single) 36″ cylinder.
1 Ditto (Trevithick's) 20″ Pole.
1 Water wheel, 25′ diameter, 4′ 11″ breast, with bobs, cranks etc.
A stamping mill, 8 heads.
2 capstans and shears.
1 9″ capstan rope, 100 fathoms (very good).
5 whims with ropes.

15 fathoms 12″ pumps	13 fathoms 9″ pumps
28 Ditto 11″ Ditto	9 Ditto 7″ Ditto
23 Ditto 10″ Ditto	
1 10″ Working barrel	1 8″ Working barrel
2 8½″ Ditto	1 5″ Ditto

With clack-seats, windbores etc. to suit.
1 11″ plunger pole, working case etc. to suit.
About 160 fathoms of shaft and bucket rods, of different sizes.
A large quantity of brass, iron, timber, miners' and smiths' tools etc.
Also all the halvans on the mine.
J. Cory, Auctioneer. Wheal Treasure, Nov. 19, 1818.

[Note: The fact that Wheal Treasure possessed a Trevithick Pole engine at this time is noteworthy. The simplicity of its design was initially thought likely to revolutionise the design of Cornish engines when first introduced in the county by Richard Trevithick in February 1816. The pump rods in the shaft were connected to a pole (20″ diameter and made of brass at Wheal Treasure) and this pole was contained within an open topped vertical cylinder or polecase situated over the shaft. Steam at a pressure of approximately 100 lbs. per square inch was admitted to the bottom of the polecase, forcing the pole upwards approximately eight feet and raising the pump rods in the shaft. The steam expanded in the polecase down to a pressure of 10 lbs. per square inch, after which the steam was exhausted and the weight of the pump rods in the shaft pulled the pole back down in the polecase, completing the working cycle. The engine could be built comparatively quickly and it did not need a large and expensive engine house. Unfortunately the pole was subject to an uneven rate of wear where it passed up and down through a sealing ring in the polecase. Steam that was intended to power the pole upwards escaped through the seal, adversely affecting the efficiency of the engine and increasing its coal consumption. Not surprisingly the pole engine soon fell out of favour.
See Francis Trevithick: Life of Richard Trevithick, 1872 and D. B. Barton: The Cornish Beam Engine, 1965.]

A subsequent advertisement on 2nd January 1819 listed the materials that were left for sale after the first auction, including the two steam engines and the Count House (mine office) furniture. Whatever the reasons were for stopping the mines Thomson told Thomas Petherick to attend the auction and buy some of the materials. Petherick spent £900 and purchased at least one of the steam engines and, apparently, most of the mine materials and the halvans. He was able therefore to leave sufficient equipment at the mine so that it could be worked again at short notice.

Meanwhile a complicated series of events which started in 1818 were souring the relationship between Austen and Thomson. In the summer of that year the two men had agreed to support a London merchant called Wildman as one of the candidates in the election for Parliament held at Fowey. Business in the town was at a low ebb,[12] and Wildman had agreed to spent £10,000 in the contest and "embark on a very considerable trade in Fowey" according to

Austen. Thomson subsequently changed his mind because he did not want the rivalry of another merchant in the locality, and they decided to switch their allegiance to Col. Alexander Glynn Campbell, the nephew of E. J. Glynn. Austen ran up large debts at the North Cornwall Bank in supporting his candidacy and fully expected to be reimbursed by Campbell. The day-to-day management of the bank was in the hands of Adam Thomson, with his partners, Glynn and Pendarves, having little knowledge of, or involvement in, the conduct of the business. According to Austen's subsequent account of the affair there was an agreement of which he was unaware between Thomson and Campbell – Campbell would not repay any expenses unless elected. Campbell had extricated Thomson from some financial difficulty in the past and this arrangement repaid the favour, Thomson telling Campbell that E. J. Glynn would assist Austen in repaying any borrowing. Campbell was defeated at the election leaving Austen heavily out of pocket. Some of the electors were not entitled to vote and there was a petition against the result, and whilst Campbell was subsequently made a Member of Parliament in 1819 he still did not repay Austen's expenses. Glynn was in no position to help Austen, and to add to their problems early in 1819 the London agents of the North Cornwall Bank threatened to withdraw their support because of the large amount of money owed to them by the 'North Cornwall'. In June 1819 Austen and the partners in the bank were making frantic efforts to keep it afloat. The difficulties were caused substantially by Austen's debts. This was largely money which Thomson had lent to him, in Thomson's capacity as the manager of the bank, to enable Austen to finance Campbell's election expenses. Austen had to mortgage some (or all) or his properties to pay money into the bank, telling Glynn on 17th June 1819 "it is a hard act for me to mortgage my estate to pay for Mr. Campbell's return to Parliament, and there I hope my connection will end with Mr. Thomson." Thomas Petherick met Thomson in Truro at the end of June and was told by him to immediately raise some money towards paying off the Wheal Treasure debt at the bank. In return Petherick asked to be reimbursed for the £900 he had spent at the auction. Thomson did not reply to this, but told Petherick to sell everything that he had purchased at the auction, including the steam engine, and to pay the proceeds in to the bank. Although Petherick stated that he would be selling 90 tons of ore from the halvans in the ensuing three weeks he was told by Thomson to sell the engine at once to the first person that made an offer for it. Petherick promised to do so but this was merely a ruse to keep Thomson happy and to stop him trying to sell the engine himself. The price of copper was low which affected its saleability and Petherick was not prepared to dispose of it at a depressed price. Arguments started between the adventurers about who was responsible for the Wheal Treasure debt at the bank, and who was actually entitled to the shares bought in Thomson's name following the meeting held in Bodmin in the summer of 1817. Thomson acknowledged that half of the shares purchased belonged to Austen, but claimed that he could not remember that Glynn was also to take an equal part.

With most of the equipment necessary to work Wheal Treasure still on the mine it appears that production started again towards the end of 1819. These were desperate times for both Austen and Thomson, the latter being described by Petherick at their meeting in Truro as appearing "very low and absent". On 1st September 1819 Thomas Robins, a partner in the East Cornwall Bank at Liskeard, wrote to William Rashleigh (Colman Rashleigh's cousin) at Menabilly: "I know that Mr. Austen's friends look upon him as a ruined man. He is greatly indebted to the North Cornwall Bank as well as to other persons." Austen referred to the continuing dispute between himself and Thomson some years later in a letter to Frederick Silver, his London solicitor and agent, underlining the problems the shareholdings were causing: "The moment the mines improved – the shares being then standing in Mr. Thomson's name in the mine books and the books being in his custody – he refused to let me have my third part and threatened to sell them all unless I would take them all. Should there be any mystery about why he would not let me have one third but the whole it is easily solved – I had other shares in the mines and by having one third standing in his name I should have a majority, but by his keeping or selling the whole I should have been in a minority." There is no indication of exactly when this took place, but on 10th December 1819 the West Briton advertised for sale a majority of shares in Wheal Treasure, Wheal Fortune, Wheal Hope and Wheal Chance and this would be consistent with Thomson's efforts to apply pressure on Austen to buy all the shares registered in his name. The problems at Wheal Treasure were not to be resolved until October 1820.

By the spring of 1820 Thomas Petherick was an active purchaser of Lanescot shares and he may well have been buying them on behalf of Austen. There was mining activity both at Lanescot and Wheal Fortune and it is apparent that Austen had managed to obtain financial backing for his mining ventures. The most likely source of money seems to have been George Lucy of Charlecote, Warwickshire who was to be elected as one of the Members of Parliament for Fowey with Austen's help in 1820. Development work at Wheal Fortune was being carried out at Blues shaft and Pidler's shaft. According to the mine's "Horse Engine Articles" which detailed the terms of the drainage contract the takers (contractors) were "to provide a proper and sufficient number of able horses to draw off the water from the bottoms[13] and to work the engine constantly during the take if required", with a fine of 2/6d for every hour that they were to cause the mine to be "hindered" by their neglect. If the taker was unable to provide horses at the required times "the Agent shall have a right to get such horses as he shall think proper to keep the water out of the mine and charge the taker with the expense of the sum in addition to the before mentioned fine of 2/6d per hour." "The Whim Drawers' Articles" stated that the taker had to provide a sufficient number of horses to "keep off the stuff" (i.e. draw the waste rock and ore out of the mine) with a fine of £1 for each time he failed to do this, with a very large penalty of £10 if he abandoned the contract altogether. Such a fate must have befallen Richard Peake who took the contract at Blues shaft on the 17th June 1820 until Midsummer 1821 at 7/- per 100 kibbles. The contract was abandoned on 20th July, and subsequently taken by John Crocker on a sliding scale:

6/- per 100 kibbles from the adit level.
7/-   ditto   from 10 fathoms under the adit.
8/-   ditto   20   ditto.
9/-   ditto   30   ditto.

The taker for the Horse Engine to unwater the mine was Capt. Sam Hitchens and partners who received £30 per month. Specialist miners called 'sump men' were sinking Blues shaft at £7.10.0. per fathom and they took the whole of August to sink the shaft just one fathom. The high price per fathom indicated the hardness of the ground, with more favourable conditions at Pidler's shaft where it was to be "sinked" by 6 men for 5 fathoms at the rate of £3 per fathom.

With production coming on stream again after the stoppage many of the individuals who were to play a very significant part in the history of the mines start to be mentioned in Austen's correspondence at about this time. His affairs were still very much centred in Fowey and William Davis, Henry Couche, Edward Remfry, James Bennetts Jnr., John Puckey and Peter Clymo were to become part of the management at Lanescot and Fowey Consols. Apart from a period in the Royal Marines from the mid 1820s to 1837 William Davis was the purser until his retirement in February 1866. Whilst he was a serving officer he was replaced by Henry Couche, and the others were mine captains, John Puckey and Peter Clymo becoming joint managers after Thomas Petherick left in the early 1830s. Eventually Clymo departed following his major discoveries at South Caradon mine near Liskeard leaving Puckey as chief agent until the latter died in 1858. For a man who was regarded with some suspicion by many of his contemporaries Austen was to retain the loyalty of some very strong characters.

Towards the end of 1820 Austen was buying shares in Lanescot in his own name. At Wheal Treasure the responsibility for the debt of £4,000 at the North Cornwall Bank evolved into a straightforward dispute between Austen and Thomson about which of them was liable to repay this borrowing. On 25th October 1820 they signed an agreement taking the dispute to arbitration, and part of this arrangement seems to have involved the mine shares because two days later Glynn and Thomson assigned their shares in Wheal Treasure, Wheal Fortune, Wheal Chance and Wheal Hope to Austen, giving him effective sole control of these mines. The North Cornwall Bank struggled on until it stopped payment in 1822. For years it had relied on the involvement of Pendarves to give it credibility, and he ultimately had to pay off its creditors. Thomson managed to come out of the matter more or less financially intact and the biggest casualty seems to have been E. J. Glynn. He was forced into bankruptcy by Pendarves in 1823 when he did not honour various financial guarantees that he had given to him. Pendarves had only just survived a financial crisis of his own before receiving an inheritance in 1815, and he subsequently became a Member of Parliament for 21 years and a member of the county establishment before dying in 1853.[14]

Notes

1. No maps have been found delineating the boundaries of the setts but they can be located from the Treffry correspondence and records at the Cornwall Records Office (CRO). Wheal Chance may not have been producing ore at this time, the only probable shaft on its sett being Trathan's.
2. J. H. Collins: Observations on the West of England Mining Region, 1912.
3. Samuel Drew: The History of Cornwall Volume II, 1824.
4. Mining Journal 5.9.1840. The Mining Journal was published weekly starting in 1835. It is still the trade paper of the mining industry. Reputed to be the oldest technical paper in the English language.
5. W. B. 9.6.1815 and 13.10.1815. The separate condenser patented by James Watt in 1768/69 enabled huge savings to be made on fuel costs. 'Double acting' steam pumping engines fell out of favour in later years because they were not as economical as 'singles'. D. B. Barton: The Cornish Beam Engine, 1965.
6. At this time it was common to have only one 'first' name, and this was often the same name as the father. The original John & Joseph Vivian appear to have been born in Camborne in the 1750s. John Vivian had two sons who were also called John & Joseph. Another John Vivian was born at Cornwood in Devon in 1749 and he became the head of the copper smelting company of Vivian & Sons. There were at least three 'John Vivians' therefore connected with Cornish mining at this time and it is impossible to say with certainty that one of the original takers of the Crinnis sett was the same person as the adventurer in Wheal Treasure. (G. C. Boase & W. P. Courtney: Bibliotheca Cornubiensis, 1878 and J. L. Vivian: The Visitations of Cornwall, 1887.) The 1794 Grant of the Crinnis sett is held at the CRO ref. CN 1984 1/2.
7. The source of the engine may have been the Perran Foundry at Perranarworthal which was established in 1791 and owned by the Fox family of Falmouth.
8. "Mr. Austen wished that they should have the management of the mine because all the ores should be carried to his wharves and Mr. Thomson should supply the materials."
   "Mr. Thomson had a very poor opinion of mining unconnected with merchandise." TF 845 & X55 at the CRO, copy letters and statements relating to a dispute between Austen and Thomson.
9. B. T. Bradfield: The Public Life of J. T. Treffry (Industrialist) of Place 1810–1850, unpublished Dissertation, University of Birmingham 1955.

10. Politics and banking are closely linked with the early history of Fowey Consols. Austen's connection with Colman Rashleigh, Walker, Pendarves and Glynn dated back to about 1809 when they were part of a small political party dedicated to reform (WB 19.7.1811). The following table may be helpful in illustrating the various relationships:

	Political Reformer	Partner in North Cornwall Bank	Adventurer in Wheal Treasure etc.
J. T. Austen	X		X
E. J. Glynn	X	X	X
E. W. W. Pendarves (Born E. W. Stackhouse)	X	X	
J. Colman Rashleigh	X		X
Rev. Robert Walker	X		X
Adam Thomson		X	X

   See W. Brian Elvins: The Reform Movement and County Politics in Cornwall 1809–1852, unpublished Thesis, University of Birmingham 1959. Copies are held at the Royal Institution of Cornwall and at the CRO.

11. TF 845 at the CRO. There is the suggestion in these papers that George Beer of Fowey had been given the contract to supply coal to Wheal Treasure to retain his political support.

12. "The trade of Fowey is at present very inconsiderable, and consists of little more than its fisheries, which of late years have been very unsuccessful." C. S. Gilbert: An Historical Survey of the County of Cornwall, 1817–1820.

13. Large iron buckets (kibbles) would have been used with a horse whim. According to William Pryce: Mineralogia Cornubiensis, 1778, they could hold 120 gallons of water. Similar buckets were used to raise ore and waste rock to the surface.

14. The Harvey records at the CRO show that Adam Thomson was still in business as a merchant in the late 1830s. John Colman Rashleigh (who was made a Baronet in 1831) left memoirs which are also held at the CRO (FS/3/1127/142), and they throw further light on his co-adventurers in Wheal Treasure. E. J. Glynn inherited family wealth and of him Colman Rashleigh said: "In the management of his own affairs he was a mere child, the dupe in succession of a number of agents who between them led him blindfold wheresoever they chose until his ruin was finally consummated by Mr. Adam Thomson, a Scotch Adventurer, whom he had accidentally fallen in with in the

north . . . he actually consented to place his affairs in this man's hands without any other inducement than pity for his extreme poverty." According to Colman Rashleigh, Pendarves's early financial problems were sufficiently severe for him to consider emigrating to avoid his creditors.

"An idea may be obtained of the different kinds of workings carried on upon a level, when driven for discovery, and when success attends the labour, by reference to the sketch, of part of Fowey Consols in which the gallery, in the distance through which a miner is proceeding with his light, was driven for discovery upon an unprofitable part of the lode; indeed, on one where it was wrung up, or nipped in, from the meeting of the walls, so that the level or gallery was driven onwards by working out a sufficient quantity of the country, or rock, on both sides. The open space, where the walls are supported by junks of timber, is where, in the progress of driving the level onwards, the lode again spread out and a bunch of ore was cut, which being cleared out, this cavity was left. The white line on the left hand is a quartzose branch, which quitted the lode in that direction.

Towards the eye, a few fathoms from the miner represented as seated, the lode again became small, but, the work of discovery having been continued, another bunch of ore was cut. It must be confessed that the sketch should not be taken as a general representation either of the height of the galleries or of the width of lodes when ore is broken. The former necessarily depends on the mode in which a mine is worked, and the expense which it may be thought advisable to incur; so that, in mines which are not very prosperous, some of these passages are very low confined places. In this sketch itself, also, the miners are represented too small as respects the gallery and open cavity, which therefore appear too large".

Sketch of underground working at Fowey Consols Mine by Sir Henry de la Beche with his comments.

CHAPTER II

DISCORD & EXPANSION

NOW THAT Austen had achieved control at Wheal Treasure and her associated mines there was an upsurge of activity at Lanescot. In November 1820 an advertisement was placed for tenders to build a steam engine boiler "about 18 feet long and 5½ feet diameter".[1] A visitor to the mine in December told Austen "they are getting on with the engine house at Lanescot and will be ready before the engineer, the new Count House will nearly be completed by next Monday, the Smith's shop is in forwardness but I believe the engine will not go to work before February or March month." There had been an improvement in Williams's lode in the 60 fathom level driven from Union shaft at Wheal Treasure, with a report of 150 tons of fine quality ore at the mine. At Wheal Fortune a lode had been cut in a crosscut driven under Pidler's shaft from the Crosspark lode, Thomas Petherick describing it as 'very kindly" and giving instructions to sink the shaft deeper. The mines were now making substantial profits, with Austen's share alone amounting to approximately £700 per month. Despite the success being achieved many of the London adventurers were unhappy with Austen's management of the mines. There was a basic conflict of interest – they were looking for the biggest financial returns, but for Austen success lay in the magnitude of his achievements and not in the size of his bank balance. Whilst some of the London investors "never saw a mine in their lives and don't know a lode from an adit" in the words of one of Austen's correspondents, others were experienced businessmen and merchants well used to investing in Cornish mines and friction was inevitable. Austen was now 38 years old and the mines had finally given him the means to make his mark in the world, and he was not going to give up that opportunity.

Frederick Silver had the unenviable task of trying to placate the London adventurers by keeping Austen's ambitions and expenditure within bounds. On the 26th March 1821, having commented on the small dividend from Lanescot "owing to the works which have been going on" he wrote to Austen "I have not had Wheal Treasure accounts but the small dividend surprises me, and our friends cannot understand the reason there is none this month, as in September above £1,500 worth of ore was sold and in October about £1,200 more and from all of which it appears that there is no more profits than £640 – this should be explained as the expenses of the mine ought to be a proportion of its produce." At Lanescot a great deal of money was being spent with little in the way of recorded ore production and only 331 tons were sold in the year to 30th June 1821. Throughout the whole of 1821 Austen continued to buy its shares, and whilst initially he did not have an overall majority he held a controlling interest and made the major decisions.

From its commencement in 1817 to the end of May 1821 the mine had made an overall loss of £6,051.[2] At the beginning of September Silver commented that "Lanescot yields her riches very slowly." Even so the shares were changing hands at £400, and with ore production increasing Austen was about to spend more money, Silver stating on the 2nd October: "I am very sorry to hear of another steam engine at Wheal Lanescot, if such shall be the case I shall certainly think the mine too rich for plenty generally makes waste, and three steam engines on one mine in three successive years speaks either of waste of money or bad management." He followed this on the 8th December: "My friends are jealous of Lanescot mine and say you forget their mines and look after Lanescot – you see the evil of having more mines than one." Whilst the heavy levels of expenditure at Lanescot may have been justifiable Silver was subsequently to accuse Austen of holding back ore production in the early part of 1821 to compel some of the London adventurers to sell out. He was still complaining in June 1822 when commenting on the mine's accounts for December 1821 to April 1822 inclusive where ore sales produced £7,600 with expenses of £6,900: "as I am not a miner the expenses compared with the returns appear very great and more so as the charges for the works at Lanescot previous to December last amounted to £10,000 and upwards – I know you had a particular reason for increasing the expenses and I presume the expenditure will in a great degree lessen the expense of all the future works." By this time Austen's continuing share purchases had enabled him to acquire 58% of the shares, giving him a majority interest.

Despite the concerns of Silver about the way the mine was being managed, production reached a record figure of 2,399 tons for the year ending 30th June 1822, and a newspaper advertisement in September for the sale of shares[3] stated that the mine had made a profit of £1,300 in the previous two months.

Ore production was also increasing at Wheal Treasure throughout 1821. There was a great deal of excitement and interest in the mines which was reflected in the share price. Whilst a 1/64th share in Wheal Fortune at £30 and Wheal Hope at £25 was little changed, a similar share in Wheal Treasure rose to £300 at one stage before falling back to £250. By the spring of 1822 Austen was moving towards the consolidation of Wheal Treasure, Wheal Fortune and Wheal Chance, his ambition since 1817. Wheal Chance was situated in the northern section of the sett and there are no records currently available to indicate the size of the workings. It seems probable that they were still small scale, and the London adventurers held few, if any, shares in it. From its commencement to the end of July 1822 Wheal Chance had made a loss of £74, and Wheal Fortune had lost £120. A major transformation had occurred at Wheal Treasure where a loss of £7,963 from commencement to Midsummer 1819 had been largely offset by a profit of £7,168 between then and the date of the consolidation of the mines,[4] ore production increasing from 766 tons for the year ended June 1821 to 2,844 tons in the following twelve months.

For accounting purposes it appears that the date of the consolidation could well have been the 1st May 1822,[5] but the adjustment of the shareholdings to effect the amalgamation continued for some months afterwards. It was evidently not popular with everyone, Silver telling Austen on 8th May "Do not be over anxious about the consolidation of the mines, for it is tiresome work to swim against the tide." With the income and output at Wheal Treasure being so much greater than that of the other mines an adventurer who had paid a high price for its shares would have been naturally reluctant to buy into Wheal Fortune and Wheal Chance in order to participate in the unifying of the mines. Their concerns would have been heightened in May when they learned that there had been a temporary standstill at Wheal Treasure (and probably Wheal Fortune) which enabled resources to be switched to Wheal Chance. It is apparent that a major discovery had been made there and development work was being carried out, Silver writing on 9th

May "I hope you have good reasons for assisting Wheal Chance, at present all the London adventurers are at a loss to know the reason and objects you have in view." There was also the suggestion of more discord at the end of the month when Austen was told by Silver "I still observe you are very sanguine in mining affairs, but surely Wheal Treasure has either been shamefully managed or the old mining trick was played off, namely get up the shares, sell out and let the buyers look like fools."

Whatever the rights and wrongs of the situation the three mines were consolidated, with total expenditure on them up to this time being £49,563.16.11.[6] On 16th. August 1822 Silver sent a letter to Austen concerning the consolidation shareholdings, and these are summarised below. Lanescot was not consolidated until 1836.

Fowey Consols		Lanescot	
Austen	39	Austen	39
Petherick	1	Petherick	1
Braham	6	Braham	4
Silver	5 ¼	Silver	4
Shears	4 ½	Shears	4
Collinson	2 ¼	Ownership	
Mahony	2	Unspecified	14
	60		66

There is a difference between these figures for the shares issued, and the shares and share prices quoted in other correspondence where, as was common for Cornish mines, they are quoted in multiples of 64. Austen subsequently purchased further shares in Fowey Consols which gave him a 72% holding, and his ownership of Lanescot shares varied between 57% and 59% at this time. The shareholdings for Austen and Petherick seem self-explanatory, Silver may have been holding shares on behalf of others, and the rest are probably 'London adventurers'.

Two notable names missing at the amalgamation are those of the Rev. Robert Walker and John Colman Rashleigh. According to the latter's account of events they had virtually given their shares in Wheal Treasure to John Hitchens, the mine captain, some time after 1818. Hitchens had then sold these shares to Austen for £10,000 almost immediately after they had been passed to him because the mine had discovered a rich lode in the meantime.[7] Another mine captain was referred to in a letter from Silver in November 1822, and a process of elimination indicates that he was probably referring to 22-year-old John Puckey: "From what I observe in Capt. P., I am bound to say that he is worthy of the confidence you place in him, in the first place he is extremely steady, an unfavourable account of the mines does not sway his ideas of the concern, a favourable account does not increase his expectations – he appears to have formed his judgments upon a general view . . . I found him in conversation strictly honourable in his views."

A newspaper advertisement on 21st September 1822[8] referred to lodes recently discovered at Fowey Consols in the east and north part of the sett, probably a "great lode at Wheal Fortune" mentioned by Silver in correpondence in July and also the discoveries at Wheal Chance. For many years after the amalgamation of the mines the old names of the setts were used to aid the identification of the various sections. Austen was now embarking on negotiations with local landowners to bring more water onto the mines to power machinery. This would make substantial cost savings and, in subsequent years, the considerable use of water power was to distinguish Lanescot and Fowey Consols from most other Cornish mines. It was necessary to use the water from Redmoor approximately three miles to the north and this needed the co-operation of Nicholas Kendall and William Rashleigh. The natural drainage of the area caused the stream from the moor and its tributaries to flow south in an approximate semi-circle passing to the east of Luxulyan at Gatty's Bridge and down through the Luxulyan Valley to Ponts Mill. A leat would have to be dug to make use of this water, and Kendall owned most of the land over which it would have to pass. He was 21 years old at the time, owned the mineral rights for a major part of the mines and was starting to receive an increasing income from the dues. He was to assist Austen over many years, but the same could not be said for William Rashleigh. None of his land was being mined but Austen was trying to obtain various setts from him, including Trenadlyn which lay at the eastern end of the Wheal Fortune lodes and Carruggatt, which lay to the north of Wheal Chance. A succession of rich lodes running mainly east-west had been intersected as the mines extended northwards up the hill, and it was reasonable to expect that this pattern would continue. Unfortunately for Austen there was a basic difference in outlook between him and Rashleigh, and in many ways this typified the clash of attitudes in the country as a whole. As a member of the landowning gentry Rashleigh appeared essentially content with things as they were, and was evidently not interested in seeing dramatic and disruptive change in the locality. Austen was a representative of the entrepreneurs and industrialists who were propelling Britain into the position of the world's greatest industrial power, albeit on the back of severe economic and social distress for some of the labouring classes. Cornwall was relatively free of the worst excesses seen in this period but both Austen and Rashleigh fully recognised that there was still great hardship for many of its inhabitants. Whilst he does not appear to have been obstructive for the sake of it, Rashleigh would not be pressurised by Austen into making decisions until he knew exactly what was involved and how it would affect him. It was not unreasonable for him to be reluctant to have his land mined, with the attendant problems of land and water pollution which would cause difficulties for his tenant farmers.

The discoveries higher up the hill in the northern part of the Fowey Consols sett had caused Austen to revise his plans for the course of the leat. Originally there had been no need to involve Rashleigh at all, but now the water was needed on the mine at a higher level it would have to be taken from further upstream than originally intended. The final plan was to bring the leat from the Ponts Mill stream at a point just below Gatty's Bridge through part of Rashleigh's estate of Greedy (Greadow) before entering Kendall's land on the north side of Luxulyan Valley. It would then follow the contours and be taken around Carmears Rocks in a launder before passing through Penpell Bottom and on to the mine by passing under the roads from St. Blazey to Lostwithiel and also under Penpillick House. The length of the leat was to be nearly three miles and when it reached Fowey Consols the topography was ideal for the use of water power. A fairly gentle slope southwards gave the water a good fall which meant that the leat could be utilized to operate a series of waterwheels as it flowed downhill. Austen set out his position in a letter to Rashleigh dated 3rd January 1823: "We never entertained a doubt about bringing the water from below Greedy to the mines, but it naturally struck us that we could afford to give to you a handsome rent for bringing the water through Greedy, in consequence of the additional fall that it would give our mines . . . for our present purpose the water will reach our mines sufficiently high to do all our work. Our mines are extending up the hill and getting deeper, and we consider that the additional fall which we should gain by the water coming through Greedy would, hereafter, be a benefit to us. Should you be inclined to have Carruggatt worked it would be a benefit to you also, as it would enable us from the adjoining land to explore subterraneously to determine whether it is worth working or not, without breaking the surface of your land. Any addition to our water fall would afford to us the means of employing many poor people, not only whilst the mines are in full working, but actually for years after the working underground is suspended, this is a fact of considerable importance to you as the principal landholder in Tywardreath, for where there is sufficient water to dress up the halvans of a mine after she ceases to work underground, the shock of what is termed her stoppage is much less felt by a Parish, because the employment does not altogether cease with the cessation of underground work.''

Austen obtained agreement from Kendall to cut the leat through his land and had started work on it in December 1822. Rashleigh was prepared to let it cross the Greedy estate giving a warning note to Thomas Robins, his steward, solicitor and banker: "with such men to deal with as the managers of Fowey Consolidated Mines requires more than common precaution." A problem arose because Rashleigh would only grant a least for the passage of the leat over his land for 7 years at a cost of £30 per annum. With the high cost of building the leat the prospect of losing the benefits after only 7 years was unacceptable to Austen, who was trying to obtain Rashleigh's agreement to increase the term of the lease by reminding him of the beneficial effects the mines were having in "giving employment to a number of poor creatures who would otherwise become a burden on their Parishes, or earn their livelihoods by dishonest means." He also inferred that he was under considerable pressure from the London adventurers to complete matters and told Rashleigh that Kendall had agreed to a 14 year lease with an option for a further 7 years and, if the mines warranted it, "we would agree to add something handsome to the present proposed rent for carrying the water through Greedy Estate during the last 7 years, if you will rent it to us for 14 years certain." Delays were evident when Austen wrote to Robins on 22nd March 1823:

"Our work on the leat immediately below Greedy of which 1/14th part has been completed has been suspended, as well as some considerable works on the mines which cannot be proceeded with until the exact height can be ascertained where we can first make use of the water. We calculate that by getting it through Greedy we should be able to effectually try that part of the mines very near your estate of Carruggatt and from a discovery made in that part of our mines last week, coupled with other favourable circumstances, it is quite clear that no part of our very extensive workings is likelier to make a great return to the adventurers and therefore every day that we take in not erecting the necessary machinery for effectively working that part of our mines is of great consequence." There is a strong probability that the activity was centred on Trathan's shaft. At the end of March a 21 year lease was completed between Austen and Kendall at a cost of £800 with an annual rent of £210 for the leat over Kendall's land, and in April Rashleigh told Robins that he was prepared to agree to Austen's terms. The paperwork was not complete in May 1823 when he wrote to Robins "I find Mr. Austen has quite an army of workmen employed in cutting the leat across Greedy. If he is doing so without your authority I suspect his plan is to get the water across my land during your absence from home, which may form the subject of future litigation." However, no legal dispute followed, and it is apparent that the matter was satisfactorily resolved despite Rashleigh's innate distrust of Austen's motives.

While success was being achieved with the leat, problems were building up for Austen in other directions. At the start of 1823 a riot occurred at the mines, and apart from the damage caused it provoked a serious dispute between Austen and John Colman Rashleigh who attended the mines in his capacity as magistrate to restore order. The cause of the riot is unknown, Austen referring to it in a letter to Colman Rashleigh on 6th February 1823 as "the conspiracy and combination of the men to bring the agents to their own terms." Austen called the disturbance a mutiny, and the men had accordingly been fined by Thomas Petherick and Bennetts, one of the mine captains. Colman Rashleigh felt that the fines levied were excessive and illegal, and he evidently showed some open sympathy towards the miners because Petherick felt his behaviour would be responsible for two or three days extra rioting. In his letter to Colman Rashleigh dated 6th February Austen stated his "expressed wish on the day after New Year's Day to see the mines stopped and all the men discharged rather than witness an illegal and triumphant mob lording it over those whom it was both their duty and interest to obey." It is worth noting that his letter to William Rashleigh referring to this section of society as "poor creatures" had been written only eight days previously. Colman Rashleigh has left his own account of a meeting with Thomas Petherick held at Prideaux House on 8th January 1823: "Received a very gross insult in the presence of my wife from Mr. Thomas Petherick in consequence of my having interfered as a Magistrate with a meeting in the mines which threatened the public peace. I sought satisfaction for it from his employer, Mr. Austen, who declined doing anything under the pretence that Mr. Thos. Petherick was the servant not of him but of the adventurers – a rich and powerful body – and whom he could not control. This appeared to me a mere shuffle in as much as Mr. Austen has a considerable majority of shares in the mine and I conceived, and still do conceive, he had the power he disclaimed."[9]

In addition to his problems with an angry workforce relations between Austen and the London adventurers were reaching a crisis against a background of falling output and declining copper prices. This was most marked at Fowey Consols where ore production fell by 32% and the sale proceeds were down 43% on the previous year in the annual figures to 30th June 1823, a decline in income of £7,805. The fall off would have been partly due to the aftermath of the riot and the need to switch labour to build the leat, but this would have affected both mines. There had been disagreement on the overall potential of the mines and whether they would prove to be rich at depth, and to many adventurers the building of the leat may have seemed an unjustified extravagance. Austen had suggested that the adventurers should pay a call on their shares to cover the cost of building the watercourse,[10] but this request had been refused. What appears to have been a general feeling of dissatisfaction culminated in a very public dispute when the adventurers accused him of overcharging for the materials, possibly coal, that he was supplying to the mines. Two London merchants, J. H. and D. T. Shears, wrote to Austen on 21st July 1823 to say that they were acting on behalf of the other adventurers, and that they had instructed the smelting companies that had recently purchased ore from Fowey Consols and Lanescot to withhold the payments that were due to him. This was a protest against the way that he was managing the mines. They followed this with a series of newspaper advertisements stating that the adventurers would no longer be responsible for any work done, or any materials supplied to the mines on the instructions of Austen or Petherick. The first advertisement appeared in the Royal Cornwall Gazette on 6th September 1823 (see copies below). The fact that John Taylor

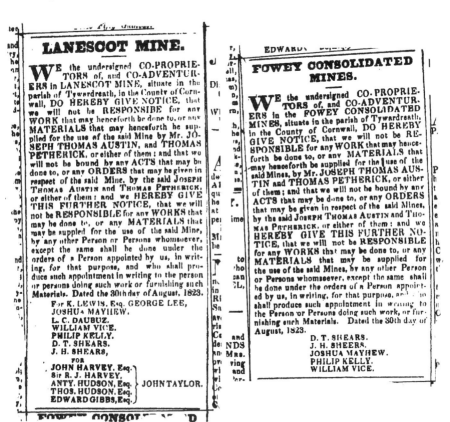

Newspaper notices of September 1823.

signed the notice on behalf of some of the Lanescot adventurers is of some significance. In 1819 he had purchased the Consolidated Mines in Gwennap and they became, for a time, the biggest copper mine in the world. He also owned shares in some of the copper mines around St. Austell Bay, and Austen was soon to become a significant rival. In response to the newspaper advertisement Austen responded with one of his own in the West Briton of 10th September in which he denied over-charging. The severity of this dispute was referred to by Austen in a letter sent to William Vice, a Truro merchant, some ten years afterwards in October 1833. Vice had originally been one of the signatories to the disclaimers in September 1823, and ironically Austen was resisting Vice's request to supply the mines with iron above the market price in 1833 when he wrote: "as soon as the London adventurers saw what was going on we should very soon find our affairs in Chancery – from which Court we were, by the correctness of our accounts, saved in 1823 when the malcontent adventurers in London examined our accounts without being able to put their finger on a single defect." The reported discovery of a rich lode of copper in the old Wheal Treasure sett in the Royal Cornwall Gazette of 9th August 1823 may have helped in resolving the dispute. However on the 23rd September Silver wrote to Austen to say "you should not expect any favour from Mr. S(hears) for although you have made peace as to the mining concern, you are mistaken if you think his opinion of you is not as fixed as ever it was."

It appears that Austen had to pay the costs of the leat himself from his already over-stretched finances. These financial problems and another labour dispute at the mines had been highlighted by Silver in March 1823 when he wrote to Austen: "I am sometimes at a loss to account for your pecuniary difficulties without considering yourself partly the cause. It is now above 18 months ago that the working of Lanescot was kept under to compel the Town Gents to sell out – then the watercourse was projected, and which two matters have filled up a long space of time unprofitably, and lately the mine has met with difficulties from these causes – viz. The meeting of the labourers (the riot), the season and now when the standard is high some dispute among the samplers stops our progress. I am anxious for the well doing of the mines on many accounts for they would silence our enemies and disconcert our pretended friends and relieve you from your pecuniary difficulties."

*The launder which took the Fowey Consols leat around the Carmears Rocks in
the Luxulyan Valley. This photograph was taken after the mine closed when the
same water supply was used to power china stone grinding mills.*

According to Nicholas Kendall, at one stage in their negotiations,[11] the use of the leat was offered by Austen to the adventurers at a rent of £200 a year, but the eventual figure agreed on was significantly higher.

The leat came on to the Fowey Consols sett in its north west corner and flowed across a small plateau to split in two near where Austen's engine house stands today, one branch flowing down the western side of the workings past Remfry's shaft and the other took water to the eastern part of the mines passing Trathan's shaft where, in 1830, a map indicates that there were at least two waterwheels.[12] There was a water whim at Remfry's shaft at this time, and perhaps both a whim and pumping engine at Trathan's operated by waterwheels. When the leat came into use is not known, but Fowey Consols put the building of two waterwheels out to tender in December 1823, one 30′ diameter x 4′ breast and the other 20′ x 6′ 8″ for completion within two months.[13] The beneficial effects of the leat bringing cheap power were seen in April 1824 when parts from two steam engines at Lanescot mine were advertised for sale by the mine's engineer, John Webb of Charlestown. A Boulton and Watt 30″ cylinder engine complete with boiler and said to be in excellent repair sold for £200, and a 36″ cylinder "with pistons and nozzles to suit" lying on Par Beach ready for shipment was also disposed of.[14] In January 1824 Fowey Consols paid its first dividend since the consolidation of the mines and in February Lanescot recommenced dividends after a similar barren period. In the year ended 30th June 1824 ore production and income was returning to the levels seen in 1822 at Fowey Consols (only to drop back again in the following twelve months). With the leat starting to prove its worth a special meeting of the adventurers in Lanescot, Wheal Hope and Fowey Consols was held at the Packhorse Inn at St. Blazey on 9th August 1824 "for the purpose of determining the compensation to be made to Joseph Thomas Austen Esq. for expenses, risk and liabilities incurred by him in respect of the Carmears Watercourse." They agreed to pay him a rental of £100 per month, and the annual income of £1,200 quickly covered the capital costs of building the leat, if not all the aggravation which accompanied it.[15]

With the difficulties of the leat behind him Austen next addressed the problem of transporting the copper ore to his ore floors and quay at Caffa Mill Pill, Fowey. The journey from the mines was approximately five miles by road, with both a steep descent to

Treesmill and ascent to the outskirts of Tywardreath before continuing to the Castledore crossroads, then lesser gradients until
the steep hill into Fowey. The ore was taken in wagons drawn by
horses or mules over roads which were totally unsuited to heavy
industrial traffic, and he planned to build a railway from the mines
to Fowey. To overcome the problems caused by the gradients near
Tywardreath the planned line ran north from the mines towards
Strickstenton, around the head of the valley and then south to
Fowey, with a big loop to follow the contours at Lantyan Wood
and a tunnel under the Castledore to Golant road en route.[16] By
September 1824 the various landowners had given their consent in
principle provided they were paid three times the value of the land
over which the line was due to pass. Thomas Graham of Penquite
had horticultural considerations uppermost in his mind when he
gave Austen permission "to carry his rail road anywhere but
through his lawn." The only landowner not to give his consent was
William Rashleigh of Menabilly, and he was waiting to see the
detailed plan of the proposed route prepared by Harry St. Aubyn
of Lostwithiel.[17] Mindful of the problems encountered with the
mine leat Rashleigh considered approaching several people connected with the mines, including John Taylor, to see whether the
adventurers gave their support to the railway. A partially completed
plan was sent to Rashleigh by Austen early in October 1824
covering the eastern part of the route between Lantyan Farm and
Caffa Mill Pill. Rashleigh was immediately concerned about the
large extent of his land through which the railway was due to pass
and the possible effect the line would have both on his farming
tenants and his own mineral rights. Meanwhile Austen was negotiat-
ing with Edward Pidler with the initial objective of obtaining a
reduction in the mineral dues paid to him in respect of the
additional machinery installed on Pidler's land in the north of the
Fowey Consols sett, but with a second objective of buying this land
at Pelean outright to enable the railway to cross it before coming
onto the mines. Pidler was not willing to co-operate, and the
discussion on the western part of the route was overtaken by events
when Rashleigh told Thomas Robins on 30th October 1824 "No
rail road will take place, but Mr. Austen must fulfil his promise of
having broad wheels – or the ores should be conveyed to the sea
at Par, instead of Fowey – I am told a quay is building for this
purpose adjoining Pembroke Mine."

The broad wheels referred to were considered to be, at least, a partial answer to the considerable damage that Austen's existing copper wagons were causing to the local roads, but he was not prepared to go to the expense of fitting wide wheels until the roads were improved. The copper mines of Gwennap used mules to carry their ores to the sea, with saddle bags slung across their backs. This was also considered to be an acceptable alternative to wagons, with the possibility of substantial numbers of mules becoming available for purchase because John Taylor was building his own railway from the Gwennap mines to Devoran. Austen told Rashleigh that no mules would become available for at least twelve months, and that their current price was too high. Austen wrote to Rashleigh on 13th November: "The objection of your tenants to the proposed rail road will no doubt encumber your parish with heavy way rates longer than it would have been desired – but neither their objection or the general use of wide wheels will be sufficient to arrest the march of science in its progress."

Austen was reluctant to give up the idea of a railway to Fowey. He had spent £2000 there improving his ore floors and quays at Caffa Mill, and in March 1825 he was receiving quay dues of 10d. per ton, with carriage costs of 6/2d. per ton for the copper ore. The local roads remained in a poor state, so much so that local farmers petitioned Rashleigh to allow the railway to proceed. Thomas Graham was particularly anxious and nervous about the condition of the roads, and it is hard to avoid the conclusion, perhaps unfairly, that he was singled out by Austen for special attention. In September 1825 Austen let it be known that he wished to ship the copper ore from Golant, which meant that his wagons would pass directly over the road to Graham's estate at Penquite. With an extremely steep road leading down to the river at Golant there must be some doubt if this was every a realistic permanent solution to the copper shipment problem, but correspondence from the time indicates that Austen's wagons did use this road for a while, much to Graham's distress. Rashleigh wrote to him: "I am truly sorry for the inconvenience that the Parish of St. Sampson (Golant) has suffered in consequence of the copper wagons passing on your roads, and it seems that the same system of annoyance is intended to be practised in your parish as was attempted to be done in Tywardreath . . . to carry the rail road into effect according to Mr. Austen's plans would be attended with much serious injury to myself and the occupiers of the soil." There is a suggestion in this letter that the roads at Tywardreath had improved, and Austen began unsuccessful negotiations with Rashleigh concerning the building of ore floors at Golant on land owned by Rashleigh. Austen's cause was not helped by the fact that he was in a long term dispute with Rashleigh over the ownership of a property at Readymoney, Fowey, known as the Battery House. Rashleigh felt that Austen had illegally taken possession of the property, telling Austen that no agreement could be reached at Golant until this dispute had been satisfactorily settled.

Whilst this matter was continuing a potential problem for Austen occurred when, in October 1825, Rashleigh gave permission to the Taylor family to search for minerals at Carruggatt. Austen was faced with the possibility that the sett would be granted to his rivals. Rashleigh's letter to Thomas Robins of 13th October gives an insight into the priorities of another age: "I am unwilling to grant any sett for mining at Carruggatt without first ascertaining the certainty of the lodes and viewing myself the precise boundaries that would be required. Mr. Taylor is welcome to direct any pits to be sunk in search of the lodes, provided he covenants to fill them in again, and make good any injury done to the tenants . . . could not a clause be inserted in the sett for preventing the carriage of ore so as to interrupt our road to church? I still hope that a rail road may be effected either to Par, or Charlestown for the conveyance of copper through the influence of the Charlestown Company and Messrs. Taylor & Co; such an event would make me more willing to grant setts." He was either referring to John Taylor or his son Richard, and if any lodes had been found Rashleigh was prepared to give father or son preference in obtaining the sett. However, like the Fowey railway, and the proposed ore floors at Golant, nothing came of it. Austen's transport problems were not resolved until he built a canal in 1829.

The period through the mid 1820s at Fowey Consols and Lanescot was characterised by a rising output and income together with labour shortages. There were also attempts to acquire adjoining setts. Trevenna was obtained from James Bower at the end of 1824 for 21 years, the terms being "dues 1/10th until the 27 fathom level (under the adit) now driving east from Mundic shaft in the land of Mr. W. Polsue in Harvey's Tenement shall be extended 25 fathoms into the estate of Trevenna and afterwards 1/12th clear of rates and taxes." Efforts made to obtain the mining rights of Trenadlyn and Great Treverran to the north of Trevenna were unsuccessful, the landowners Rashleigh and Richard Foster of Castle, Lostwithiel, refusing permission in 1827 for Austen to divert the stream which flowed through Carruggatt Wood so it would flow across Colwith to Great Treverran "for the purpose of trying the lodes on that estate." The two men stated that they wished to retain their rights to the stream in case it was needed "for working any mines that may hereafter be discovered in our lands adjoining, particularly Carruggatt." According to Austen's calculations the main Fowey Consols leat was saving the mines £10,000 per year in fuel and steam engine costs. However the increasing depth and extent of the underground workings was leading to a greater need for more pumping machinery and a growing demand on the water supply which provided the source of power. This supply was inherently erratic, and fell off badly in dry summers. An indication of the increasing depth at Lanescot can be obtained by comparing a brief report from Thomas Petherick in June 1824 when he refers to "new pitches under the 50 fathom level west of Sampson's shaft extending west of Coates's . . . the lode in the 50 fathom level west of Tremayne's shaft is 5' by 3' – worth £16 per fathom" with a full summary of the same mine compiled by William Petherick, Thomas Petherick's brother, on 6th October 1828:-

"Reported by Peter Clymo Jnr.: Bone's lode in the 90 fathom level east of Tremayne's shaft is 3 feet big, orey and kindly. The Crosspark lode in the 70 fathom level east of Sampson's shaft is in two parts, the north part is about 15 ins. big and the south part 1 foot big, will turn out two tons per fathom. The Crosspark lode in the 80 fathom level east of Sampson's shaft is 2 feet big, coarse work. The south part of the Crosspark lode in the 80 fathom level east of Sampson's shaft is 2 feet big and will turn out 1 ½ tons per fathom. Reported by James Bennetts Jnr.: Williams's lode in the 60 fathom level east of Union shaft is very small and poor. Cook's lode in the 33 fathom level west of Union shaft is 1 foot big and good work, it will turn out about 1 ½ tons per fathom. Cook's lode in the 22 fathom level east of Union shaft is about 6 ins. big, very poor but good ground. Reported by William Petherick: The lode in the 80 fathom level on the south part of the Crosspark lode east of Sampson's shaft is about 2 feet big and will turn out about 2 tons per fathom."[18]

A comparison of the income and output from Lanescot and Fowey Consols for the two years in question underlines their relative growth:

	Year ended 30.6.1824		Year ended 30.6.1828	
	Tons of ore	Proceeds £	Tons of ore	Proceeds £
Lanescot	2,390	14,548	7,500	41,248
Fowey Consols	2,634	15,906	4,216	23,494

Like any other business the mines were vulnerable to events elsewhere, and these caused a financial and practical problem for Austen when their profitable progress was interrupted for a short time towards the end of 1826.[19]

In December 1825 the worst financial crisis since the South Sea Bubble[20] of 1720 hit the City of London. A sustained period of headlong growth and speculation ended in a financial crash as confidence evaporated, leaving merchants with stock that they could not sell and banks with loans that could not be repaid. Dozens of London and country banks subsequently failed after suffering runs, and a general economic recession ensued throughout the country. By August the copper ore price had nearly halved to £3.12.0 per ton, causing a short term financial loss to Fowey Consols until prices recovered again towards the end of the year. The country banks took much of the blame for the crisis, and were subsequently forbidden to issue their £1 and £2 notes which were thought to be a partial cause of instability. In February 1828 Austen wrote to Robert Peel, the Home Secretary, to complain that "a great part of the labouring class will be thrown out of employment the moment that the local one pound notes cease to circulate." The banks could continue to issue £5 notes, but he felt that these were too large for the payment of wages and that "either the labourer will ruin himself by daily going into debt for the necessaries of life for the maintenance of himself and family until he has earned so much as five pounds from his employer, or the employer, by paying weekly so many of them together as may have earned five pounds, will be the indirect cause of driving them to the nearest public house to change the bill, divide, and, I might add, spend the proceeds!" This must have been a major practical problem for the mines, with Austen giving the number of his employees in a letter to George Lucy in

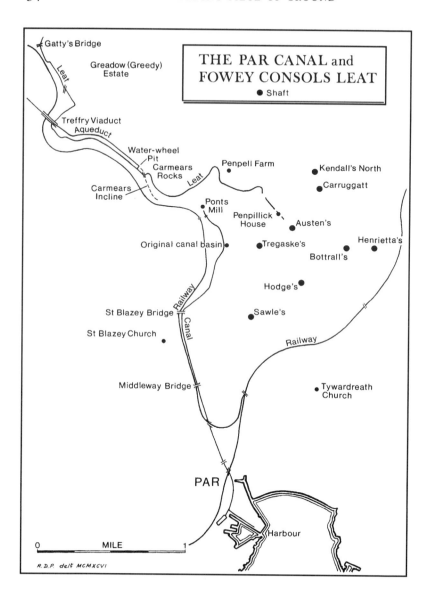

Gatty's Bridge

Greadow (Greedy)
Estate

Leat

**THE PAR CANAL and
FOWEY CONSOLS LEAT**

● Shaft

Treffry Viaduct
Aqueduct

Water-wheel
Pit
Carmears
Rocks

Penpell Farm

Kendall's North

Carruggatt

Carmears
Incline

Leat

Ponts
Mill

Penpillick
House

Austen's

Henrietta's

Original canal basin

Tregaske's

Bottrall's

Hodge's

Railway

St Blazey Bridge

Canal

Sawle's

St Blazey Church

Railway

Middleway Bridge

Tywardreath
Church

PAR

Harbour

0   MILE   1

R.D.P. delf MCMXCVI

Map showing routes of Leats, the Par Canal and the present railway.

January 1828: "In Fowey nearly all the trade and employment are derived from me – the poor of St. Sampson (Golant) are employed in my mines – and in Tywardreath I not only employ upwards of 1100 people but pay about one half of the rates of the whole parish." By 1828 all able bodied men at Fowey Consols and Lanescot were required to work underground or be dismissed,[21] the problem continuing from 1825 when Thomas Petherick stated that the working of the mines was "considerably impeded by the scarcity of miners, owing principally to the want of dwelling houses in the neighbourhood."

In 1826 the combined output of the two mines placed them fifth in the list of Cornish copper producers behind the Consolidated Mines in Gwennap, East Crinnis, Dolcoath and Pembroke mines, of which East Crinnis and Pembroke were less than three miles away. In 1827 they rose to second place, a position they were to occupy for many years behind Gwennap Consols. Whatever Austen's hopes were when he gained control of the mines it seems probable that their output exceeded his most optimistic expectations. The doubters had been silenced, and the end of 1828 saw the mines about to enter a new era of investment and expansion.

Notes

1. RCG 4.11.1820.
2. John Keast: The King of Mid Cornwall, 1982.
3. RCG 21.9.1822.
4. "The King of Mid Cornwall" and Mining Journal 3.10.1840.
5. RCG 1.6.1822.
6. MJ 5.9.1840.
7. Memoirs of Sir John Colman Rashleigh. John Hitchens used part of the money to purchase the manor of St. Blazey from him for £6,000. "Lake's Parochial History of Cornwall" states that the manor comprised nearly the whole town of St. Blazey, and according to C. S. Gilbert's "Historical Survey of Cornwall" at that time it contained only "a parish church, two small inns and a few other dwellings."
8. RCG.
9. Memoirs of Sir John Colman Rashleigh. CRO FS/3/1127.
10. MJ 29.8.1840.
11. RCG 1.8.1851.
12. Held at Royal Institution of Cornwall, Truro ref HJ/8/5214.
13. West Briton 12.12.1823.

14. RCG 3.4.1824. The sale of the engine is detailed in the Account Book held at the CRO, ref X 55/14.
15. In his book "The King of Mid Cornwall" John Keast gives the total cost of the leat at £3,850, the main items being £1,860 for leases of land, £370.2.9 for stores, £615.3.2 for labour, £81.8.9 for carpentry with compensation for land (damaged) at £75.10.0. He also mentions a rental of £800 to Nicholas Kendall which may have been the premium paid for the lease.
16. Plan held at the CRO ref X484 1/2.
17. St. Aubyn also examined the route of the Pentewan Railway in 1828. M. J. T. Lewis: The Pentewan Railway, 1981.
18. It is possible that Sampson's shaft at Lanescot was named after Benjamin Sampson (c. 1770–1840), and this would indicate a continuing connection with the Perran Foundry. Sampson rose from being a carpenter at Tresavean Mine near Lanner to become the manager and resident partner of the foundry for the Fox family, and eventual sole owner of the Kennall Vale Gunpowder factory at Ponsanooth. Lanescot mine purchased its powder from the Kennall Gunpowder Co. in the early 1820s.
19. John Keast: The King of Mid Cornwall.
20. A rapid rise in the share price of the South Sea Company set off a speculative boom which quickly collapsed. The company had bribed several members of the government and confidence in the financial structure of the country was undermined.
21. RCG 3.4.1830 A miner called Manley refused to comply with this order and was dismissed. To gain his revenge together with others he pulled down part of the Fowey Consols leat, and subsequently received 12 months hard labour when caught.

CHAPTER III

THE GREAT ENGINE AND THE SEPARATOR

AUSTEN BUILT a canal about two miles long from near the foot of Penpillick Hill to the sea at Par in 1829. The increasing output of ore from Lanescot and Fowey Consols would have led to a growing need to improve its transport to the coast, and at the same time provided him with the money to pay for the canal and to start to build the harbour and breakwater at Par. He and Colman Rashleigh had examined the proposed route as early as 1818, and despite his previous efforts to build a railway to Fowey Austen opted for a canal as the best means of moving the ore and supplies, not-withstanding heavier construction and trans-shipment costs. He was in good company, with several canals either being built or recently opened in the south west of England at this time, the nearest being the Liskeard and Looe Union Canal which was fully opened in 1828. He turned to Robert Coad, the engineer for the Liskeard and Looe,[1] for advice and by the end of May the canal was said to be "in rapid progress." It followed the original route of the Par river from below Ponts Mill to St. Blazey Bridge[2] where a reservoir was built for the canal, and from there a totally new channel was dug which ran in a virtual straight line to Par past Middleway Bridge.[3] The canal originally terminated at a basin in the valley to the west of Tregaske's shaft. Austen wrote to George Lucy on 2nd August 1829: "I have very nearly finished my canal and yesterday launched the first boat to go on her – the boat will be drawn by one horse and will carry as much at one time as can be drawn on my wagons by 16 horses. I have in addition to my canal, which from the rapidity of its execution appears to have been produced by magic, begun a large breakwater across the sea to protect vessels entering to collect the copper ores at the mouth of the canal, and if I can accomplish that object I have no doubt in my own mind it will save the mines in the carriage of ores above four thousand pounds a year." In later years the canal was extended to terminate at Ponts Mill and the Mining Journal of 25th May 1844 provided a description of it: "There are three locks, each 90 feet long, and with a fall in two of 5 feet each, making together a rise of 10 feet from high water mark to the foot of the inclined plane, the third being a tidal lock. The boats employed are calculated to carry 52 tons, which are drawn by one horse. There is a feeder of water to scour the canal, or to fill it when occasion may require. The water used is from springs, the mine water being too objectionable on account of its sediment or deposit." An inclined plane was built from the canal basin to the waste burrows adjoining Tregaske's shaft, and a tramway was constructed from there to Lanescot mine so ore could be transported to the canal boats. The specifications and cost of the incline were given as "Height 80 feet, length 1,127 feet – forming and finishing the plane, arching the tunnel (under the St. Blazey to Lostwithiel road), and all materials, including the short regulating lever, stage and ropes £630."[4] The plane was self acting, i.e. the weight of the descending tram wagon pulled up an empty wagon. The savings were substantial, with the quay dues and transport costs to Fowey of 7/- per ton in 1825 reduced to 4/6d. per ton by 1839 when the canal to Par had been in use for ten years. Austen immediately passed these savings on to the adventurers even though he paid the building costs of the canal himself. The canal was replaced by a tramway in 1851.[5]

The year ended 30th June 1829 marked the peak of production for Lanescot mine at 7,864 tons of ore, far in excess of the 4,859 tons produced at Fowey Consols. The dressing of the ore brought to the surface involved sorting it into material suitable for smelting or to be discarded as waste. (More general detail is given in Chapter V.) Much of this work was carried out by women and children and there was a shortage of such labour at the mines.[6] Jigging the ore was carried out by boys to separate some of the finer sized ore from the waste found with it in the lode. The fine material was placed in a hand held sieve which was moved up and down in a hutch or box of water. Copper ore had a higher specific gravity than the waste so that the ore gradually settled on the lower part of the sieve and a waste layer could be skimmed off the top. From 1828 onwards Thomas Petherick set out to mechanise this process, improve the quality of separation and reduce the manual labour involved.

Earlier work to improve jigging, largely in the Derbyshire lead

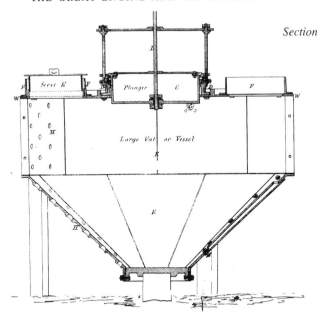

Section

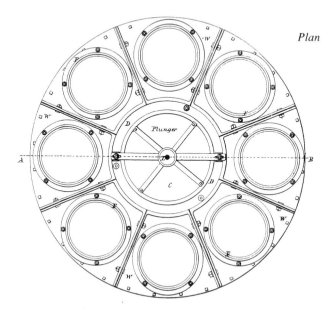

Plan

Drawing of a separator from the 1830 patent.

district, had used levers on which the sieve was hung enabling operators to work larger jigs. Petherick went further than this and kept the sieve stationary but moved the water up and down by the use of a plunger worked mechanically. He took out a patent for this in 1830.[7] The new jigging machine was called a 'separator' and consisted of a large container with a plunger in the middle. The container was filled with water to a point just below a lid which covered it. The lid had circular holes to accommodate up to eight sieves filled with material to be dressed and these were placed with the bottom of the sieve just above the level of water in the container. The plunger was moved up and down by a rod activated by a rocking beam driven by a crank on a flywheel. The flywheel was driven by a waterwheel at Fowey Consols and Lanescot although the patent refers to the alternative prime movers of steam, horses, or manpower. The motion of the plunger caused the water to rise through the sieves and then fall back again, replicating the action of the hand held sieve. When a sieve in the separator had "layered" the sieves were removed by hand and replaced by other sieves which were then filled from a hopper. This meant that the boy was no longer working the sieve in water but was filling and emptying sieves which he placed in and took out of the separator. It was claimed that one boy could do the work of three and with more efficiency.

Thomas Petherick evidently worked hard on this process because in 1832[7] he took out another patent to cover further improvements to mechanical jigging. His new patent sought to produce a more effective jigging action by one of two methods. His first was to use a one way valve in the plunger arranged so that the upward stroke of the plunger was effective in allowing the water to raise the materials in the sieve, but in the downward stroke the one way valve opened and the material was allowed to fall naturally by gravity. His second improvement was an alternative method where, instead of a plunger, a surge of water from a cistern was used to lift material in the sieve. The surge was achieved by opening and then closing a valve from the cistern. He specified that valve operation could be manual or by machinery. This method used more water than his other method.

Writing in 1831 in the Quarterly Mining Review John Taylor described Petherick's separator as "very ingenious". Robert Hunt, a campaigner for the professional education of miners, reported an experiment at Fowey Consols involving 300 tons of copper ore which was divided in two, with one half treated by hand jigging and the other half by the separator. This showed that the separator produced a higher quality product at a reduced labour cost.[8]

The use of this new machinery was referred to by John Farey when describing the water driven machinery on the two mines in 1831:[9] "There were three or four large overshot water wheels for pumping water out of the mines, also several other overshot water wheels, some of them for drawing up ore out of the mines; others for crushing ore, for stamping ore, for dressing ore by machinery then newly invented by Mr. Thomas Petherick, and one for sawing timber. The supply of water for all the machinery is brought from a considerable distance by artificial water course (the Fowey Consols Leat) whereby a constant stream is delivered into a reservoir or mill dam, which is embanked at some height above ground where the mines are situated; and the ground beneath which the mines extend having a considerable slope downwards towards the river allows large overshot water wheels to be employed at four successive falls or steps; the same water, after turning one set of such wheels, running away to turn others situated further down the slope, and then others still lower, and so on in the usual manner of water mills. The mines were formerly drained by an adit intersecting the lodes at 40 fathoms below the surface in the principal part of the workings, but they were afterwards excavated below the adit, deepening progressively until one part had reached a depth of 123 fathoms in 1831; the drainage of those excavations below the adit was effected at first by pumps worked by the overshot water wheels above mentioned,[10] and afterwards by the additional aid of water pressure engines, activated by letting down portions of the water from several mill dams." At this time there were five water pressure engines underground to assist with the drainage of the mines, all of which were installed some time after 1825. They were considered a more effective way of pumping water than the use of water wheels. Whilst a Cornish beam engine used the power of steam acting on a piston to raise the main pump rod in the shaft, a water pressure engine was installed in the shaft itself just above the adit level and it used the weight of a column of water to operate the piston. Farey described the 22½″ water pressure engine in Union shaft as having a piston stroke of 6 feet with a column of water 41 fathoms high weighing 40,595 lbs. to operate it. The column of water was fed

Sketch of Surface Scene with Separators. Published in The Saturday Magazine of 1st February 1834.

from a cistern 20 feet above the surface, and at each stroke the engine raised 30,558 lbs. of water out of the mine.[11] The water in the column drained away through an adit at the end of the stroke. (A full description of the workings of a water pressure engine is given in Appendix V with diagrams.)

Despite the emphasis placed on water power at the mines it is clear that if steam power was ever totally discontinued then it was only for a short time. The first engines from Fowey Consols and Lanescot to appear in a Cornish publication called Lean's Engine Reporter[12] are a 40″ single pumping engine erected on Union shaft which appeared for the first time in the edition for May 1831 and a 21″ single pumping engine which was situated on Ray's shaft and recorded between November 1831 and August 1832, after which it was presumably taken down and disposed of. The 40″ was ordered from Harvey & Co of Hayle in October 1825 at a cost of £800 and delivered in the summer of 1826. The financial problems at Fowey Consols that autumn caused a delay in paying the bill. This engine shared Union shaft with the 22½″ water pressure engine and the pump rod from the 40″ steam engine could be connected to the pump rod of the water pressure engine for use when there was insufficient water available to operate the water pressure engine.[13] It is quite probable that the 21″ steam pumping engine at Ray's shaft had also been on the mine for a considerable time before appearing in the publication, and in addition to these two steam engines there was at least one other which was referred to in correspondence as "our old steam whim". These engines were under the control of the mines' engineer, John Webb, who had designed as well as ordered a 24″ water pressure engine for Fowey Consols which was supplied by Harveys in 1829. Webb served as engineer on several mines in the 1820s, and whilst little is known about him today entries in Lean's Engine Reporter indicate that he assisted some of the foremost Cornish engineers of the time. In 1820 he was an engineer at Crinnis and the neighbouring Cuddra mine working with Arthur Woolf and William Sims respectively, and subsequently he was also engineer at Herland Mine in Gwinear where he worked on two large 80″ cylinder pumping engines. It is not known when he was appointed at Fowey Consols but he was in this post by 1824, and doubtless his knowledge of the Herland engines was used when Thomas Petherick made initial enquiries to Harvey's foundry in February 1831 concerning the building of an

80″ pumping engine for Fowey Consols. Adventurers often sought a reduction in the mineral dues paid to landowners when they made significant investments in a mine, and this proposed new engine would have featured in the negotiations concerning such a reduction and referred to by Austen in a letter dated 12th January 1831, stating that the "Lords in Lanescot and Fowey Consols, notwithstanding the dividends which we are making, have reduced our dues one quarter part and Mr. Tremayne,[14] who is largely concerned in mines in the west, declared that he never saw any ground so well tried as our mines and his mining agent said he never saw any ground so well worked below the surface."

Austen's plans were about to be interrupted. Years of hard times and misery for many culminated in large-scale social unrest throughout England in the autumn of 1830, with riots, rick burning, the destruction of agricultural machinery and threats to landowners commonplace throughout the southern counties.[15] The West Briton of 24th December 1830 reported on a meeting at Callington "to consider the best means of alleviating the distresses of the poor which are daily increasing in that parish" and "we also understand that the miners employed in the neighbourhood of St. Austell and Fowey have again threatened to prevent the shipment of corn in the neighbouring ports of Fowey and Charlestown etc." On 19th February 1831 Edward Remfry, a miner of St. Blazey, was tied on an ass with placards reading "I am the Black Sheep of East Crinnis mine" tied to his back and chest. He was led the four miles from Tywardreath to St. Austell Bridge on the animal, accompanied by 500 miners who objected to the fact that he took a pitch at East Crinnis while he already had one at Pembroke mine.[16] The following Tuesday 3,000 miners marched through Helston "in perfect order" to prevent further shipments of corn from the town. This was also the setting day at Fowey Consols and Lanescot which the miners attended with the aim of controlling the bidding for pitches to ensure that the prices were kept up. (Tribute and tutwork pitches went to the lowest bidder.) Two men refused to join in this arrangement and they took refuge in the Count House when threatened by the other men. The miners refused to disperse and magistrates, including Austen and Nicholas Kendall, were called in and the Riot Act was read. The men still did not leave and seven of the rioters were arrested, and according to the Royal Cornwall Gazette "on their being put into chaises for conveyance to prison, a violent attempt to rescue the prisoners was made by several hundred persons present; but by the temperate and firm conduct of the civil power, they were enabled after a conflict of more than an hour to forward the prisoners to Bodmin, in persuance of their commitment." The next day large numbers of miners met on Par Green and it was reported that they intended to go to Bodmin to free their colleagues. The High Sheriff of Cornwall and neighbouring magistrates went to Bodmin to swear in between 30 and 40 special constables and the Royal Cornwall Militia was called out. On Thursday evening it was rumoured that the miners were approaching Bodmin. The Militiamen were armed and placed inside the prison and the constables were assembled in readiness. The townspeople barricaded their houses in anticipation of a large and angry horde of miners. At six o'clock a motley crowd mainly consisting of women and children entered the town, and on the advice of the inhabitants they sent a deputation to see the Sheriff, J. H. Tremayne, at the jail. They were each given a pint of beer and a penny loaf and sent back to their companions who were all persuaded to leave Bodmin and return home. Some days later a Scottish Regiment was landed at Fowey and marched up to the mines, presumably as a reminder to the miners of the likely consequences of another disturbance.[17]

The seven men arrested during the riot were tried at the Lent Assizes at Launceston in March with "having committed a Riot at Fowey Consols and Lanescot mines, in the Parish of Tywardreath, and with having refused to disperse at the end of one hour after the Riot Act had been duly read", for which they faced the death penalty. However the Judge was "persuaded that great mischief has been done by the speeches and writings of base and designing men, inflaming the lower orders against the more wealthy, by statements charging the rich with want of kindness and with bad treatment to the poor." The seven men were discharged after receiving a lengthy lecture, and were told "You will not allow your minds to be disturbed by any of those wicked persons who are travelling about the country, deluding the ignorant and unwary, by encouraging them to impose conditions upon their employers."[18] The riot had serious financial consequences for Austen, and the disruption caused can be gauged from a letter he wrote to Richard Leane, his shipping agent, on 8th July 1831: "I believe that I told you of the great falling off from our mines in consequence of the riots – at least £6,000 since February and Mr. Petherick has just informed me that we do not yet know the worst of it. With such an unexpected loss, and being obliged to employ nearly 200 people at Par and in the (Luxulyan) quarries to make Par (harbour) safe against winter I shall not be able to purchase anything that I can properly do without, until I can reduce my expenses at Par.''

In 1831 William West came to Fowey Consols and Lanescot to eventually take over as the engineer for the mines. According to Lean's Engine Reporter, John Webb continued in the post until March 1832 when he was superseded by William Petherick and West as joint engineers, and West became the sole engineer when the former left the mines after 1837.[19] West was born in 1801 at Dolcoath mine in Camborne where his father was in charge of the farm on the sett. He had very little formal education but he was highly ambitious and shrewd with great engineering ability. According to his obituary: "bluff, blunt, hearty, outspoken, he despised everything that savoured of mere politeness and make-believe. He always called a spade a spade, and if he thought a thing said it, utterly regardless of the consequences."[20] West was recommended to Austen following three years spent at Wheal Towan at Porthtowan as deputy engineer there.

The shaft for the proposed 80″ pumping engine was in the course of sinking in the winter of 1831/32. It was situated on the northern boundary of the productive ground at Fowey Consols, with the intention of developing a northern extension should the Carruggatt sett be granted by William Rashleigh. The main shaft (Austen's) was perpendicular from the surface, with a separate shaft sunk alongside for hauling ore and materials. This was the best mining practice but extremely expensive. In October 1831 Thomas Petherick was asked for a valuation of the materials on the mines, presumably to set before Austen's bankers. According to an approximate estimate from Petherick the "machinery, erections, stores, tools etc." at Fowey Consols, Lanescot and Wheal Hope were worth from £18,000 to £19,000 to the adventurers, with the halvans worth an additional £3,000. In July 1832 Austen valued his own stake in the mine materials at £30,000, and "to this add the present price that Fowey Consols shares are selling at and my shares in that mine are worth about £20,000 more. In this calculation the shares are valued at less than three years purchase. I have said nothing of the value of Lanescot shares because none have been sold in the last year". The ore production at Lanescot was declining at this time which probably made the shares less saleable, and the statement seems to indicate Fowey Consols was paying an annual dividend of about £10,000.

Attention had switched from the northern to the southern part of the mines when Austen wrote on 19th April 1832: "In consequence of a great discovery at Lanescot mine about six weeks ago we have been making an extraordinary rush to get up machinery for getting to work there in June and lately the standard has improved. From the appearance of the new discovery we are likely to have a new mine in that part of the sett altogether." This related to discoveries at Sawle's shaft which lay over ½ mile away from the central part of the mines and about 225 yards southwest of Seymour's shaft. A 24" single pumping engine was erected on Sawle's shaft by Petherick and West, but with the costs of all the work being undertaken, including sinking Austen's shafts and the development work at Sawle's section, the mines were financially stretched. In November 1832 Austen wrote to Thomas Robins who was a partner in the East Cornwall Bank requesting an increase in his bill discounting facility of £500 per week, referring to "a great increase in tutwork at Fowey Consols and Lanescot mines where, during the last three months, we have had to reconstruct one of our steam engines (the old steam whim) to build one entire new engine which is now just ready to go to work in drawing the ores to surface from some of our recent discoveries (at Trathen's shaft), and we are making preparations for the erection of an immense stamping mill which we hope to set to work by the middle of next month on ores which ought to have been in the course of returning (i.e. the ore dressed and sold) for upwards of two years past. These operations including the buildings still in progress near another new steam engine erected within the last six months for pumping the water at Sawle's shaft have not only caused a scarcity of workmen in that neighbourhood but greatly added to our expenditure, our pay this day, for instance, at the mines alone has been £1,360, on this day week it was £1,400 and in neither were included lords dues, dividends, merchants bills or parochial rates. Now, as a necessary consequence of so much additional machinery we expect a great increase in our returns, but it will require some months to bring them round, and therefore during the present winter there will be a certain drawback on our present returns." The request was not granted.[21] The increase in tutwork is an indication of the amount of exploratory and development work being undertaken to allow the mines to be worked efficiently and the set of stamps was being erected to process the hundreds of tons of poorer quality ores left untreated at the mines' surface. This was, at least partially, made up of residues from the crushing machines which needed to be further reduced in size for additional processing. The stamps machinery ordered from Harveys specified wrought iron lifters instead of wood, and this was one of the first instances in Cornwall where they were used.[22] Another roll crusher was also ordered from them (known as 'The Great Crushing Machine') with 3' 10" diameter barrels and they also supplied the replacement parts for the old steam whim which was re-erected on Trathan's shaft with a 20" cylinder.

Harveys continued to benefit from major investments in new machinery. A new 18" whim engine was ordered from them and installed between Ray's and Pidler's shafts to wind out of both. Known as Ray's engine it was due to be at work by the end of October 1832, but was delayed because cholera affected the Hayle foundry. William Petherick and West were rushed off to the foundry in January 1833 when the double water wheel whim broke. This wheel was situated between Union shaft and Sampson's shaft and wound out of both, and it was the only one of its type ever known to have been erected in Cornwall. Instead of having all the buckets facing in one direction around the circumference the buckets around the left hand side of the circumference faced in the opposite direction to those on the right. The wheel could therefore be made to operate in a clockwise or anti-clockwise direction depending upon the side to which the water was directed, and Austen stated that "the repair of it, without delay, is of the utmost consequence to Fowey Consols and Lanescot." (This wheel is shown on the Fowey Consols plan from de la Beche on page 63 marked 'double wheel water whim'.) At about this time another 18" steam whim was erected north of Union shaft to wind out of both Powne's shaft and Union shaft (known as Powne's engine), presumably as a precaution against a similar emergency occurring again in this area of the mines.

On 6th April 1833 William Petherick wrote to Harvey & Co finally ordering the 80" steam pumping engine which was designed by West and due to be placed on Austen's shaft. The cost was

£1,975, and the order stated that "for this price the articles are to be of the very best quality, and the workmanship such as will enable us to vie with any other engine in the county." At this time Lean's Engine Reporter was the focus of intense rivalry between Cornish engineers due to its reporting of duty figures on a monthly basis. Duty was expressed as the number of pounds weight of water lifted one foot high by burning one bushel (94 lbs.) of coal. This gave a general indication of the efficiency of the engine, but not the power which was directly related to the size of the cylinder. In practice large engines with cylinders of 80″ diameter usually topped the duty list, and whilst the Engine Reporter did not include all the engines in the county its monthly comparisons provided widely available evidence of who was building the outstanding engines of the day. This had clear implications in terms of prestige for the mines on which they stood and increased business for the engineers that designed them. When mines wished to have an engine reported Capt. Thomas Lean installed a counter on it to record the number of strokes made by the engine, and the counter was secured by a lock to which Lean held the key. He measured the pumps' capacity per stroke and at the end of the month he calculated the average duty for the period from the number of strokes made by the engine, the water raised and the coal consumed. Average duty figures for the engines quoted in the Reporter rose throughout the late 1820s, one of the most successful being an 80″ at Wheal Towan which averaged duty of 77.3 million throughout 1828, with a peak figure of 87 million for the April of that year. The high duty was ascribed to an increased boiler pressure of 40 lbs. per square inch and improved insulation of steam pipes and boilers. During this period the engineer at Wheal Towan was Capt. Samuel Grose, and William West was his assistant.

The 80″ pumping engine ordered for Fowey Consols was five times as powerful as the 40″ engine on Union shaft and had more capacity than immediately needed by the mine. However, Austen's shaft was calculated to cut the principal lode of the mine at 290 fathoms below the surface and the engine had to be sufficiently big to drain the mine at even greater depths. The engine did provide a short term benefit insofar as it superseded some of the water pressure engines, enabling the water they used to be freed for use in processing the ores and powering the various water wheels at the surface.[23]

After a wet winter of frustrating delay the 80″ finally went to work on Saturday 3rd May 1834, and whilst it replaced the 40″ steam engine at Union shaft the 22½″ water pressure engine remained there. The starting of the 80″ was publicised in the Royal Cornwall Gazette, and in July it appeared in the Engine Reporter with a duty figure of 90 million, the highest figure for any engine that month. By September the figure had risen to a record figure of 97,856,382 and in the words of the proprietors of the Reporter "This created great astonishment among the miners and engineers of other mines, accompanied with suspicions, which were openly declared, that some deception had been practiced to cause the appearance of such an extraordinary performance; and the adventurers were called upon to submit the engine to a trial before disinterested and unprejudiced men, who should either verify or disprove the statement. Mr. Austen, the principal proprietor of Fowey Consols mine, immediately responded to the call." The trial eventually took place in October 1835, long enough for the mine to train the engine men thoroughly and ensure that nothing was left to chance. Through his shipping interests Austen also had access to the very best Welsh steam coal. A committee of seven persons "unconnected with the mine" was appointed to oversee the trial, one of whose number was Thomas Petherick. As the brother of William Petherick and Austen's right-hand man through the early troubled history of the mines his inclusion seems to stretch the definition of "unconnected", even though he was no longer employed at Fowey Consols. The average duty for the engine in the period from January to September 1835 inclusive was 90.9 million, and in the trial which lasted for 24 hours and 27 minutes between 22nd and 23rd October the engine averaged 4.29 strokes per minute pulling from 131 fathoms and performed a duty of 125,095,713. This set off a great controversy in the Cornish engineering world, led initially by James Sims, another engineer, who had expressed an interest in designing the engine himself. He contended that a 24 hour period was too short to be a fair trial, and pointed out that the committee was not made up of practical engineers, reservations shared by many of his colleagues. A contemporary and independent opinion on the engine can be obtained from the writings of Thomas Wicksteed, who was sent to Cornwall by the directors of the East London Water Works to examine the performance of the best Cornish engines. Austen's 80″ was, in his opinion, the most impressive engine in Cornwall and

We, the undersigned, having been appointed a Committee to conduct the trial of Austen's Engine, make the following Report of our proceedings, and the result of the experiment.

STATEMENT OF PROCEEDINGS.

1st—The Coal-Sheds carefully examined and found to be quite empty.

2nd—Twenty-eight Bushels of Coals measured in the presence of the Committee and others.

3rd—A Bushel of Coals weighed, and found to be 94lb.

4th—The Coal Shed door immediately locked, the key kept by the Committee and the door scaled.

5th—The Committee's Counter at starting registered 00,000,000, and Mr. Lean, the Reporter's Counter, 62,187,480. The Counters locked and sealed as soon as their state was ascertained, and the keys delivered to the Chairman of the Committee.

6th—Quantity of Grease delivered for the consumption of the Engine 12lbs, and Oil 1 quart.

7th—State of the Fires strictly examined.

8th—Water in the Boilers found to be at the regular working guage.

9th—Steam Guage at starting 36½.

10th—Stroke in the shaft 9 feet 3 inches.

The Trial commenced on Thursday, at 28 minutes after 1 o'clock, P.M.

During the Trial, which lasted 24 hours and 27 minutes, the Steam Guage fluctuated between 36½ and 45, shewing a pressure of from 36½ to 45 lbs. on every square inch of the Boilers; and the length of stroke in the shaft ranged from 9 feet 3 inches to 9 feet 5 inches, but the duty has been calculated at the minimum of 9 feet 3 inches.

The exact quantity of Coals consumed was twenty-four bushels.

On unlocking and unsealing the Counters in the presence of every Member of the Committee, their respective states were found to be as follow, viz:—

<blockquote>
Committee's Counter registered   6947
Mr. Lean, the Reporter's Counter, registered 2193767
</blockquote>

Shewing that the Engine made 6287 strokes, which is found to be 4,29 strokes per minute.

The working of the Lilly Lift was suspended, in consequence of the prang of the bucket breaking, and this Lift remained idle from 40 minutes past Seven o'clock in the Evening, to 23 minutes past Ten o'clock at Night, being 2 hours and 43 minutes, for which stoppage, 3 hours have been allowed in the calculation of duty.

The Steam Guage at the termination of the trial stood at 44, being 7½ more than at the beginning.

CALCULATION.

	fath. ft.	inch.		lbs.
Tye, Rose, and Crown Lifts,	97 3 and 15	Box	44870,96
Lilly Lift	20 3 and 10¼	Box	4405,84
Puppy Lift	13 3 and 10¼	Box	2901,06

$$52177,36$$

Deduct for Lilly Lift being idle ⅛ of the whole }   551,00
time of working   }

$$51626,36$$

Duty, 125,695,713 lbs. raised one foot high by a Bushel of Coals,

Four Bushels of Coals remained unconsumed at the conclusion of the experiment, making the whole consumption 24 bushels.

At the time the Engine stopped, the Fires were in equally as good, if not better, condition, than at the commencement of the investigation.

The water in the Boilers was higher at the conclusion than at the commencement of the experiment.

(Signed)   JOHN BUDGE, Chairman,
                    SAM. LYLE,
                    THOS. PETHERICK,
                    JOHN BRAY,
                    JAMES THOMAS,
                    WILLIAM REMFRY,
                    JOSEPH MORCOM, Jun.

Pitmen appointed by the Committee for examining the Pump Work,

JOHN PASCOE, from Herland Mines.
MARK JAMES, from Tamar Consols.
SAMUEL SECOMB, from Holmbush Mines.
SAMUEL HENWOOD, from Holmbush Mines.
RICHARD BENNETT, from Valletort Consols.
THOMAS RODDA, from the Tavistock Mining Company,

Report of Austen's Engine Trial 1835.
Reproduced by kind permission of the Royal Institution of Cornwall.

he found that "the construction of the valves and other parts of the engine is so perfect that although its load was equal to 51,000 lbs. the hand gear might be worked by a boy of 10 years of age as far as strength was required . . . there was scarcely any noise, the greatest was that of the steam in its passage through the expansion valve. To one who had been used to the noise of the pumping engines in London, it appeared remarkable."[24]

The most obvious difference between Austens 80″ and other Cornish engines at that time was the use of a lattice work beam, but in Wicksteed's view the superior performance of the engine was due to the design of the boilers and the high level of insulation of Cornish engines in general. However this particular design of boiler was discontinued after a few years because it proved troublesome. It caused the feed water to be heated rapidly and "transgressed the principle that the coolest feed water should meet the coolest gasses."[25] In the following years the use of a duty figure to judge an engine fell in importance. The consumption of coal was not always accurately measured, much depended on the frictional resistance in the pumps, and operating an engine to achieve a high duty tended to put an unacceptable strain on both pumps and engine.[26] However the trial of October 1835 is regarded as an excellent achievement even if the actual duty figure was accomplished under special conditions. It led to a recognition of West's abilities and expanded his career beyond the boundaries of Cornwall.

While this engine was being ordered and installed other significant developments were taking place. Austen obtained permission from the local landowners to build an incline and tunnel from the canal basin west of Tregaske's shaft to the new engine house. John Cock granted the right "to rut (cut), form and make a tunnel" to Austen on 1st November 1834[27] at the peppercorn rent of 5/- per annum, and the construction must have started shortly afterwards. The incline rose a total of 280 feet with a length of 2,640 feet including the tunnel which was 840 feet long, measuring 9′ by 9′, with two shafts in the tunnel admitting light and air. The cost of building this was £1,619 and the installation of a 30 horse-power water wheel at the top of the incline with the associated ropes and machinery cost an additional £1,200.[28] Whereas the southern incline built five years earlier was designed to transport ore downhill to the canal, the new incline was installed to bring coal and materials up from the canal basin, with a 10 ton load being wound up by the water wheel in 15 minutes. The installation of the stamps nearby at Wheal Hope probably dates from 1834 when opinions were being sought for "the best and cheapest way of dressing the large burrow of leavings near the Porcupine (Inn)." It was recommended that the mine "should build a light stamps, every head should be about 100 lbs, and each head should be lifted about 64 times a minute – our reason for having the heads so light is on account of the burrow (material) being already of a reduced size, consequently it does not require a heavy head." The ore production at Fowey Consols was increasing steadily, and whilst the discoveries at Sawle's shaft temporarily halted Lanescot's decline this was only a short term reprieve. From 1822 until 1832 Lanescot had paid dividends totalling £45,000,[29] but subsequently it made losses and with the price obtained for its ores falling and its output dropping rapidly it was decided to amalgamate it with Fowey Consols. The last parcel of ore it sold as a separate mine was 81 tons sold at the Truro ticketing on 25th February 1836. Copper continued to be produced from the Lanescot sett however, and the 24″ pumping engine on Sawle's shaft continued to work until May 1838 and it was advertised for sale in June 1838.[30] The Lanescot adventurers seem to have had the choice of either taking shares in the new consolidation of both mines or receiving compensation from Fowey Consols for the value of the materials left on the old Lanescot sett, where much of the ore dressing machinery was situated. Austen took 362 of the 512 shares issued at the consolidation (70.7%).

William Davis returned to the mines at about this time to replace Henry Couche as purser. He continued to serve as a major in the Royal Marines at Plymouth until he was able to resign from his post there towards the end of 1837. On a very large mine like Fowey Consols the purser was often a man of very high status and authority, second only to the chief captain or agent. He not only acted as a paid employee but also as a middle man in dealing with the financial affairs of the mine, making his own arrangements with the adventurers and conducting his own bank accounts for its transactions. He was required to give a proper statement of the mines' finances at the 'Account' meetings. With this amount of freedom the mine was very dependant on his honesty and competence, and the few remaining items of correspondence from the time show that Couche left some major financial problems behind him when he departed. It appears that the payments due to the Lanescot adventurers were withheld pending Couche sorting out his affairs with the Fowey Consols adventurers, and if the former ever received their money then it was not for several years. On 27th April 1837 Davis wrote to Austen from Plymouth to say "I am sorry to learn that Mr. Couche has not been at the mines to make up his accounts since I left, and that Mr. Hennah refuses to assist him unless promised to be paid by the adventurers." Austen subsequently wrote to William Tweedy of the Cornish Bank in Truro referring to "the very large sum of money" owed to the Lanescot adventurers by Couche, and to the employment of solicitors "to compel Mr. Couche to close his accounts with the Fowey Consols adventurers since when he appears to be in earnest about making his books up." On 21st. March 1839 he told a solicitor "With regard to the value of the materials belonging to your client in the late Lanescot mine – the amount whatever it may be ought to have been paid long ago – but the late purser Mr. Couche has never yet closed his accounts and there is a large balance standing against him, and as all the adventurers (who have attended the mines' meetings) have seen the correspondence they are satisfied that I have done my utmost to get the business settled. Indeed, lately he has been working hard at making up his books. It is an affair of public notoriety to all the adventurers and as soon as he is able to produce a balance sheet all those concerned will have due notice of it." The last available letter on the subject is dated 29th November 1840 and was sent to Austen by a 70-year-old stating "I must get the money due to me so long for the sale of the materials of the Lanescot mine . . . you have twice written on the subject of Mr. Couche with whom I can have nothing to do. A mine agent, be he drunk or sober, is of course answerable to the person who employed him and the person who is head of a mining concern is of course answerable for the agents he employs."[31]

In the year to 31st December 1836 the income of the two mines peaked at £100,204 and although the production of ore was higher in the next two years the proceeds never reached this figure again. Whilst this is a comparatively small figure by modern standards it has to be seen against the values of the time, when the best paid miners were earning £3.12.0. per month. There were now nearly 1,700 people employed at Fowey Consols, and the complexities of running a venture of this size are indicated in a letter sent to Austen by Davis in April 1836. It is interesting not only for its content but also for the direct way in which he instructs his formidable employer: "I wish you to look at Fowey Consols Tutwork and Tribute books to see if they are kept up close and what their average gettings may now be and also the Counting House Expenses Book and Wine and Spirit Expenditure Book to ascertain what the expenditure might have been, by whom ordered, and on what occasions. Also call for the Bankers' Accounts, to see that the transactions are regularly entered up and balanced separately every Monday and credit given in your account for the several sums received from them. This you will learn from the references where credited, being noted in red ink; also ensure that the Cash Books are kept close up and with all possible references affixed by Tuesday morning in each week. Also call for the book containing all the particulars of your Cash and Bill transactions with and through the mines and see that the folio where entered either to your debit or credit as the case may be noted in the spare column for that purpose. Mr. Hennah will give you all the books and 20 minutes, or at most half an hour, will accomplish all that is really essential for you to do; for I only care about you examining and exercising control over the books first named. The knowledge that the others are to be placed before you for examination will ensure their being got ready, and I shall be able to examine them, for which I shall give the necessary instructions to Mr. Hennah." Edward Hennah was, it seems, a clerk in the Count House and not one of Davis's favourites as another letter to Austen dated 1st July 1837 shows: "I think, for many reasons, it will be desirable to let Mr. Hennah fill Mr. Hale's vacancy – one who can fill the situation more effectively cannot be found, but unless Capt. Francis is particular with him to begin, so as to ensure a punctual attendance when the boys and girls go to work in the morning there will be trouble in getting him to break through his lazy habits."

In the early part of the nineteenth century Cornish Count House dinners were notable for hearty eating and sometimes notorious for the heavy consumption of alcohol. At one dinner on the mine early in 1838 75 people sat down to dine in the Count House dining room and a further 26 dined in the Map room. The menu consisted of boiled and roast beef and mutton. An unspecified amount of cider was drunk together with a total of seven gallons of gin, rum and brandy.[32] It is understandable that Davis should again suggest to

Austen "I think it would not be amiss if you were occasionally to call for the Counting House Expenses Book, and the Wines and Spirits Expenditure Book, where you will see every expenditure of liquor specified and the knowledge that you look at those books would tend to curtail many items of expenditure."

Notes

1. M. J. Messenger: Caradon & Looe – The Canal, Railways and Mines, 1978.
2. Cornwall Archaeological Unit: The Luxulyan Valley, 1988.
3. It ran parallel to a diversion of the river which had been made circa 1780 from St. Blazey Bridge to Par. RCG 15.4.1853.
4. RCG 2.2.1844.
5. On 28.5.1851 it was said "The canal being found ill-adapted and inadequate for the traffic a railway is now in course of formation and indeed nearly completed to run parallel with the canal". TF 1056 at the CRO.
6. Austen wrote to the Overseers of Fowey on 5th February 1829: "Much work may no doubt be done with advantage to the Parish within the walls of the Parish House, but if you have any paupers able to get their living out of doors, I think it necessary to say that I will find employment, at good wages, for any number of boys, girls or women at the mines."
7. The 1830 patent is numbered 5935, the 1832 patent is No. 6239.
8. Quarterly Mining Review, 1832. Hunt was made Lecturer on Mechanical Sciences when the Government School of Mines was established in 1851. He visited Fowey Consols in November 1860 to promote the professional education of miners. RCG 23.11.1860.
9. A Treatise on the Steam Engine, Vol. II, first published 1827.
10. Pumping water out of a mine was effected by using a main pump rod which ran from the top of the shaft to the bottom with offset plunger poles running parallel to the rod. The water wheel, water pressure engine or steam engine lifted the rod in the shaft approximately nine or ten feet and the pump rod was then allowed to descend slowly under its own weight, the plunger poles attached to it forcing water up through a series of valves from one cistern to another in the shaft until it was raised sufficiently high to run away through the adit. The pump rod became longer and heavier the deeper the shaft became, and in a deep shaft the rod and its attachments could weigh 150 tons. To counterbalance part of this weight balance bobs or boxes were installed at surface and in the shaft, consisting of a beam which was connected to

the main rod at one end and the other end was weighted with iron or stone as a counterbalance.

11. John Farey: A Treatise on the Steam Engine.
12. The Reporter started publication early in the nineteenth century and compared the size and performance of selected Cornish engines. It also gave other technical details and the name of the various mine engineers.
13. John Farey: A Treatise on the Steam Engine.
14. John Hearle Tremayne, who inherited the Tremayne estates from the Rev. H. H. Tremayne who died in February 1829.
15. "Economic misery, pauperism, starvation and class injustice had brought society to the verge of dissolution." G. M. Trevelyan: British History in the Nineteenth Century, 1928.
16. WB 25.2.1831.
17. RCG 21.2.1831. The Regiment involved was the 73rd Foot, the forerunner of the 2nd Battalion The Black Watch. I am indebted to Maurice Cooke for this information.
18. WB 1.4.1831.
19. There were three Petherick brothers connected with Fowey Consols, the sons of John Petherick Snr. who came from Trevarth in the copper mining parish of Gwennap. Thomas and William are known to have played a significant part in the history of the mine, and the subsequent careers of the brothers mirrors the nomadic lives of many Cornish miners.

	Year of birth	Left Fowey Consols	Known subsequent career
Thomas Petherick	1794	Early 1830s	Emigrated to U.S.A. circa 1843.
John Petherick Jnr.	1803	1832	Knockmahon Mines, Waterford, Ireland. Emigrated to Tuscany, Italy circa 1852.
William Petherick	1804	1838(?)	Armagh, Ireland. U.S.A. Par Consols (1862).

(Information obtained from Bibliotheca Cornubiensis, the Harvey papers and the Parliamentary Commission on health and safety in non-coal mines, Report published 1864).

There appear to be at least two other contemporary 'William Pethericks'. One was the Manager at Dolcoath mine from 1822 to 1844 (T. R. Harris: Dolcoath, Queen of Cornish Mines, 1974) and the Census

of 1851 shows his namesake was the Manager of the Devon & Cornwall
Bank at High Cross Street, St. Austell. From published dates of births
and deaths it seems that they were separate individuals.

20. MJ 2.6.1879.
21. On 1.1.1834 Thomas Robins wrote to William Rashleigh: "I have always
avoided having more to do with Mr. Austen than has been absolutely
necessary . . . he is a desperate speculator."
22. R. Hunt: British Mining, 1884.
23. RCG 10.5.1834.
24. MJ 30.12.1837.
25. R. J. Law: The Boilers of Richard Trevithick and Arthur Woolf. Journal
of the Trevithick Society No. 9 (1982).
26. Engines were operated at a high degree of expansion and the use of a
short cut off meant imposing a very rapid acceleration early in the piston
stroke.
27. TF 2907 at the CRO.
28. RCG 2.2.1844.
29. MJ 31.3.1849.
30. MJ 9.6.1838.
31. At the time of the 1851 Census Couche was 52 years old, living in Fore
St., Fowey and trading as a ship broker and coal merchant.
32. The Diaries of William Pease held at the CRO. (DDX 715).

CHAPTER IV

EASTERN EXTENSION

SINCE 1834 Austen had been continuing his efforts to expand the size of the Fowey Consols sett. In that year William Rashleigh was finally persuaded to permit mining at Carruggatt, but was undecided whether to grant the sett to Austen or the East Crinnis adventurers who had sunk their prospecting (costeaning) pits there in 1827. As well as Richard Taylor the other East Crinnis men involved were John Rundle, M.P. for Tavistock in 1835, and a John(?) Gill. Rundle and Gill had assisted Rashleigh in sorting out a legal problem at Biscovey Moor near East Crinnis mine, and Rashleigh was in a dilemma whether to repay this favour by granting Carruggatt to them or to Austen, who he knew had long been interested in the sett and was better placed to work it. Rundle suggested to Rashleigh that the sett should be granted jointly to himself and Austen, and this was agreed together with a similar joint ownership of the neighbouring sett of Colwith which was granted to them by Richard Foster. This started a debate between Austen, Rundle and Foster on the best way of mining Carruggatt and the proposed course of a deep adit to be driven into the sett. In May 1835 Austen had started mining operations at what became Par Consols, his other large mine in the St. Blazey area two miles to the south west of Fowey Consols. The fact that this sett was taken from under the noses of the East Crinnis adventurers whose mine lay nearby may have had some bearing on the future course of events. Rundle and his partners proceeded to acquire the setts of Little Treverran and Trenadlyn to the east of Fowey Consols and various setts to the west, causing Austen to state later that they had "pretty well surrounded Fowey Consols mine." On 29th November 1836 he wrote to Rashleigh to say that "whatever lodes we may cut in Carruggatt and Colwith will run through Little Treverran and therefore the latter estate ought to be united to the other two. Ask any man who understands mining and he will tell you that in the interest of all parties such a union ought to have taken place, but as Messrs. Rundle and Co. are working Little Treverran, if you think that they will work it effectively independent of Carruggatt, I would not wish by any means to interfere, although according to the usual courtesy upon such occasions the workings of Little Treverran ought only to have been undertaken in union with Carruggatt. But with regard to Trenadlyn, as I before informed you, Messrs. Rundle & Co. after merely putting down a few (costeaning) pits abandoned the place; nor is that to be wondered at (by those) who know how they have worked ground elsewhere. The fact is that as Trenadlyn is directly on the run of the lodes in Fowey Consols mine, on common courtesy Messrs. Rundle & Co. ought not to have applied for any sett there . . . as the lodes dip on the opposite hill there does not appear any reasonable prospect of ore being discovered until the lodes are explored at about 100 fathoms below the adit, for which reason an engine of very great power is required even in comparison with the power of other engines."

An engine shaft to develop the area, called Henrietta's, had started sinking on the eastern edge of the Fowey Consols sett where it adjoined Trenadlyn. Austen had sent Rashleigh an estimate of the costs at £16,616 covering the installation of the engine, sinking the shaft and the development work underground. Today when diamond core drills are used for assessing an ore body this is a reminder of the huge financial risks undertaken in the metal mines of the time, when it could take years and a very large sum of money to explore an ore body with no guarantee of a successful conclusion. The similarities between the events at Henrietta's shaft and those which occurred at Austen's shaft 1,000 yards away and up the hill to the north west are quite striking. In each case the shaft was sunk near land owned by Rashleigh where Austen wished to acquire the sett, and on both occasions Thomas Robins was left in no doubt by Austen that he was the best person to work the sett. Both engine shafts had separate whim shafts sunk alongside, and the similarities were intended to extend to the engine which was due to be erected at Henrietta's. In 1835/36 Harveys built an 80″ pumping engine for the East Cornwall Silver Mine near Callington to exactly the same design as the 80″ on Austen's shaft. This engine was due to be sold at auction in June 1837 and the prospectus stated that "the engine was erected about twelve months since, in the most improved principle, by Mr. West." The auction took place at a time of national recession following a boom the previous year, and Austen wished to buy the 80″ but only if he could obtain it cheaply. However Fowey Consols was not successful at the auction,[1] and it was to be another 2½ years before an engine was erected at Henrietta's shaft. Eventually an agreed method of working Carruggatt was found, and it appears that Austen later managed to obtain the Trenadlyn sett from Rashleigh after it had been given up by the East Crinnis adventurers.

In the spring of 1837 Henry T. de la Beche, Director of the Ordnance Geological Survey, visited Fowey Consols to obtain information for his book "A Report on the Geology of Cornwall, Devon and West Somerset" which was published in 1839. He told Austen that he was "particularly anxious to engrave your surface plan because the works are decidedly the best by far as to their general arrangement; in many of the Cornish mines the works can scarcely be said to have any arrangements at all, being rather a series of patches added from time to time as the mine progressed in any given direction." In his book he mentioned the high cost of tutwork needed to develop a mine, stating "Perhaps Fowey Consols may be cited as the best existing example in the district of the value of a constant system of working for discovery; so that, from having a large amount of ground open, from which a great quantity of copper ores are on the whole raised, expenses are incurred for discovery which would be ruinous if this mine were split up into three or four smaller adventures; for, from time to time, the search being attended with success in various parts of the mine, as a whole, a constant profit is kept up." Referring to the often erratic nature of mineral lodes and the way they sometimes dwindled away in the surrounding country rock before opening out again he reported "Carn Brea (mine) is a recent instance of workings having been abandoned in consequence of the wringing up of a lode, or, in other words, the close contact of walls for some distance, and afterwards turning out a rich and profitable mine by continuing the workings through the space so wrung up, until the lode became larger, or, in other words, the original fissure became wider, where a rich bunch of ore was cut . . . Minor instances in many mines might be noticed; in Fowey Consols, where so much skill and judgment have been exhibited, there are several, so that, if this mine had not been worked on the large scale which it has been, numerous rich bunches of ore never could have been cut."[2] He also noted that the lodes in the mine ran generally west to east, the ore shoots dipping deeper towards the east. An advertisement for the sale of part of the mineral rights of the mine at Pelean in the north eastern part of the sett in August 1837[3] referred to "the eastern and most productive part of Fowey Consols copper mine."

A full report sent by John Puckey to Austen in London and dated 15th April 1837 indicates the level of activity east of the road from Penpillick to Treesmill. The produce referred to in the letter below is the percentage of copper metal in the ore, malleable copper is native copper or copper found in its pure state and gozzan or gossan is the rust coloured oxidised capping in a mineral lode: "I understand at Bottrall's the bottom ends both east and west are not so good as when you left notwithstanding the lode is large and kindly and from the west end saving work, at the 100 fathoms level the west end viz. coming towards Pidler's shaft is still somewhat disordered. At the east end the lode is considerably improved, it has been very small in the last 15 fathoms, but is now 3½ feet big with every indication of there being an orey and large lode for some way before us. The other ends at Bottrall's are much the same as they have been for the last month. The lode is not so good in the end at the 110 west of Remfry's shaft but is still kindly. At the 110 end east of Pidler's viz. on the Crosspark lode going towards Bottrall's the lode is still very good, I must beg to remark here that there is a chance of this course of ore holding up to the south of the 100 fathoms level, even to the levels above which we shall very shortly be able to prove. The lodes in the other ends, shafts, winzes etc. are just as usual. Our tribute setting yesterday was very good taking into account the standard which fell on Thursday £4.18.0. making the standard on that day £102.3.0. and produce 8 (%). The parcel of ore 108 tons brought £5.8.0, the 105 tons £4.14.0, the 101 tons Sawle's stamps ore £2.6.0, the 91 tons £5.1.6, all bought by four companies making with the carriage £1,867.0.3. In consequence of the very low produce of Sawle's ore our ores sold to within 7/6d of the average of the county, Carn Brea and other ores . . . we shall sample on Monday next 3 parcels of ore, 94 tons about 6 produce, 93 tons about 8 produce and a further 91 tons about 8½ produce, all of which at the present standard will make, carriage inclusive, about £1,400. I believe there is no doubt in raising 300 tons a week for the next two samplings. I should have said before that the 20 end east of West's shaft is not so rich for malleable copper as it was (this is when the stone produced 140 ozs. of silver to the ton).

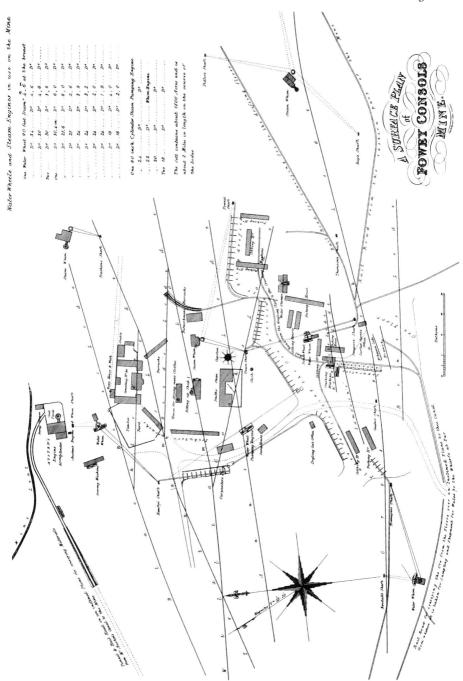

Plan of Mine drawn in 1837. (See note on page 64).

NOTES ON THE DE LA BECHE PLAN & TRANSVERSE SECTION OF FOWEY CONSOLS MINE

Plans of the mine were being requested by Sir Henry de la Beche in 1837, and this is probably a map of the mine at the end of that year. The steam winding engines (whims) were in a period of change and the plan shows an 18″ engine (known as Powne's engine) situated to the north of Union shaft and winding from both Union and Powne's shafts. The winding drum or cage revolved horizontally which facilitated winding from more than one shaft. In 1838 this engine was due to be removed and replaced by a 22″ whim which was installed in a new engine house on the eastern edge of Powne's shaft. Ray's 18″ whim engine is shown equidistant from Ray's and Pidler's shafts and was able to wind from both as well as another shaft to the east which was possibly Bottrall's. This shaft was probably down to the 110 fathom level at the time and a 22″ whim engine (Davis's) was erected on the shaft at the end of 1837. Together with Sawle's 24″ pumping engine this engine is listed amongst the steam engines but is not shown on the plan. The road between Trathans 20″ whim engine and its shaft is not shown, and the cutting and tunnel to the south west of the shaft probably indicates that the ore was landed at a plat underground and trammed out from there.

At the surface the transverse section shows the soon to be removed whim engine (Powne's) to the north of Union shaft. The lodes generally slope or underlie to the north, with Sampson's shaft vertical to the 10 fathom level after which it follows the Crosspark lode on the underlie to the 80 fathom level.

The plan and section first appeared in a Report on the Geology of Cornwall, Devon & West Somerset by Sir Henry de la Beche in 1839. They are reproduced courtesy of the British Geological Survey.

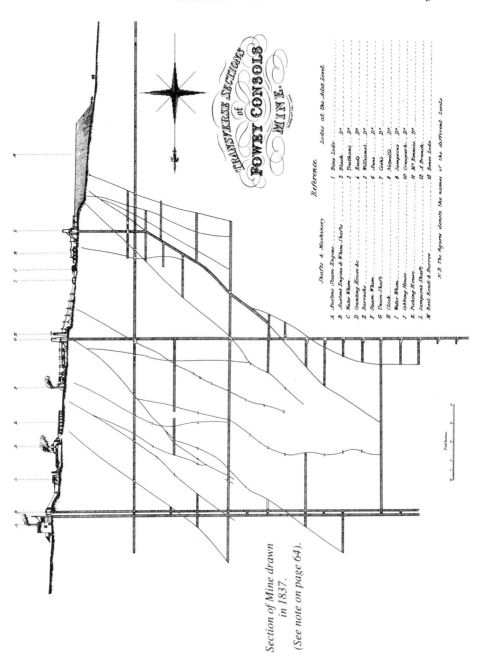

Section of Mine drawn
in 1837.
(See note on page 64).

Reference. Lodes at the Adit Level.

Shafts & Machinery.

A. Austens Steam Engine.
B. Austens Engine & Wham Shafts
C. Water Wham.
D. Counting House &c.
E. Barracks.
F. Steam Wham.
G. Union Shaft.
H. Clock.
I. Water Wham.
J. Gibbing House.
K. Picking House.
L. Sampsons Shaft.
M. Rail Road & Burrow.

1. Bica Lode. D°
2. Black. D°
3. Trethani. D°
4. Radis. D°
5. Williams. D°
6. Ann. D°
7. Cocks. D°
8. Netwells. D°
9. Sampsons. D°
10. Crowspark. D°
11. M° Kennie. D°
12. A Branch.
13. Bonee Lode.

N.B. The figures denote the names of the different Lodes

Fathoms

The men that work there told me today that two feet of the south part of the lode was comprised chiefly of gozzan."

Although it is known that silver was found at Fowey Consols no figures are available showing the amount produced. It may have been quite significant because, soon after 1837, Austen built a smelting works at Par. This was best known for smelting lead ores to yield lead and silver, but for seven years up to 1847 he experimented with smelting copper ores using coal brought from South Wales. This was not a commercial success, and in a letter to Parliament he stated that the loss suffered would have been considerably greater but for the silver recovered from the Fowey Consols ores.[4]

The most significant event at the mine in 1837 was probably the decision to go deeper into the old Lanescot sett by driving crosscuts south from Wheal Treasure. On 1st November 1837 the mineral lords agreed to reduce their dues at Lanescot from 1/16th to 1/30th in consideration of two cross cuts proposed to be driven south. One was at the 180 fathoms level from Union shaft to cut Jeffrey's lode or other branches and the second was from the 160 fathom level from Remfry's shaft to cut Bone's lode. The reduction in dues was to continue until the losses made in the last few years of Lanescot mine were recouped, and after that the payments were to continue at 1/20th. A letter sent by John Puckey to Austen in September referred to the probable cost of the crosscut from Union shaft at £1,000 and "I would observe that the mine since the dues were reduced to 1/30th had been very expensively worked in sinking and opening ground on tutwork but this ground had not turned out to expectation." The letter indicates that the dues had already been reduced on an informal basis before the official agreement had been signed. Whilst the mine continued to maintain its production of ore the disappointing results were not a severe problem, but this was a hint of difficulties to come.

The year of 1838 marked the high point in the history of the mine and it was notable for Austen himself. He was made High Sheriff of Cornwall for the year and on 14th February he took the family name of Treffry, William Rashleigh congratulating him "on taking the highly respectable name of your ancestors." He is accordingly referred to as Treffry in the following text.

A report to the Adventurers of Fowey Consols mine was published on 23rd March 1839[5] covering the year of 1838 and giving details of the output and income over the period 1834 to 1838, with the dividends from Fowey Consols alone amounting to £61,952 in this period. Ore production at 15,771 tons reached a level which was never equalled again, and dividends paid to the adventurers in Fowey Consols and Lanescot from the start of the mines were quoted at £145,238. The machinery was listed in the report as follows:-

WATER WHEELS

Name of Wheel	Diameter	Breadth	Horse Power	Remarks
Union	34'	4' 6"	52	Pumping engine
Remfry's	30'	3' 6"	32	For drawing ores etc. to surface
Old Stamps	19'	4'	22	For stamping halvans
Timber Sawing	27'	2' 6"	18	Using 12 vertical & circular saws
Sampson's	24'	3'	27	For drawing ores etc. to surface
Old Grinder	24'	3' 8"	30	For crushing & pulverising ores
Separator	24'	1' 9"	15	For jigging or cleansing ores
Great Grinder	27' 6"	6'	60	For stamping and pulverising ores
Wheal Hope	40'	3' 6"	60	For stamping halvans
New Stamps	30' 4"	6'	65	For stamping halvans
Tremayne's	24'	4'	27	For drawing ores etc. to surface
Fitting Up	14'	2' 6"	5	For turning lathes, boring etc.
New Separator	12'	1' 6"	4	For jigging or cleansing ores
Total Horse Power by Water Wheels			417	

STEAM ENGINES

	Cylinder dia.	Action	Horse Power	
Austen's	80"	Single	200	Pumping engine
Henrietta's	80"	Single	200	In course of erection
Davis's	22"	Double	30	For drawing ores

Powne's	22″	Double	30	For drawing ores
Ditto	18″	Double	15	Superseded by the foregoing more powerful engine and to be removed to another part of the mine after undergoing a thorough repair
Trathan's	20″	Double	22	For drawing ores
Ray's	18″	Double	15	For drawing ores

HYDRAULIC (Water Pressure) ENGINES

	Column dia.	Horse power	Height of column of water in fathoms
Bottrall's	24″	49	30
Union	22½″	52	45

There were significant developments in the eastern part of the mine where a 24″ water pressure engine had been placed in Bottrall's shaft and a 22″ steam whim erected there at the end of 1837. This was ordered from Harveys at a cost of £500, and whereas most engines on Cornish mines took their name from the shaft on which they stood this one was named Davis's, no doubt to mark the return of William Davis to the mine as purser. The increasing depth of the workings and the need for greater hauling power had led to the replacement of the 18″ whim on Powne's shaft by a 22″ whim obtained from Harveys in October 1838, built to exactly the same design as Davis's whim but at an increased cost of £525.[6] Although the mine report states that the redundant 18″ whim was to be removed to another part of the mine it is probable that it was eventually taken to Par Consols. Whilst it was not mentioned in the report Austen's engine had been pumping out of two shafts since May 1837, the power transmitted to the other shaft by 120 fathoms of flat rods at surface.[7] The second shaft used for pumping seems to have been either Trathan's or Union which fall more or less on the correct radius. It seems logical to suggest that perhaps the flat rods could be connected to the water pressure engine pump rods in Union shaft as the 40″ pumping engine previously at the shaft had been several years earlier. The proposed 80″ pumping engine said in the 1838 report to be in the course of erection on Henrietta's shaft was not placed there until 1840. The following extract from the report illustrates the complex undertaking that Fowey Consols had become:-

The following is a Synopsis of the quantity of Ores raised, and also the *Proceeds* and *Expenditure* of the FOWEY CONSOLS MINE, in the parish of Tywardreath, in the county of Cornwall, for one year, ending the 31st December, 1838; together with a *Statistical Account* of the number of persons employed, their average monthly wages, &c.:-

	Tons	Cwt.	Qrs.
Quantity of ores raised within the above time	15,771	7	0

	£.	*s.*	d.
Amount of proceeds for ores sold, including the carriage-money paid for the same	95,190	8	9
Total amount of expenses for the year	76,691	16	3
Amount of profit in 1838	£18,498	12	6
Amount paid to the adventurers in six dividends	17,408	0	0
Amount added to the reserved fund	£1,090	12	6

The expenses may be divided under the following heads, viz:-

	£.	*s.*	d.
Amount of agency, including purser, clerks, and storekeeper	£1,428	13	6
" Lord's Dish, or dues, &c.	5,510	2	7
" smithery (including boiler and chain-makers)	1,179	2	3
" carpentry and sawing	730	2	4
" masonry	183	10	4
" pitwork, timberwork, and capstaning	808	0	0
" mapping, dialling, &c.	170	2	0
" engineer, and engine-men working pumping-engines, and rent of water	1,656	3	2
" tutwork, or work underground in prosecuting a mine for discovering ore, by driving levels, &c.	14,718	6	8
" tribute, or underground work, in extracting ores when discovered or laid open	21,825	15	6
" sundry surface labour, and sundries	1,727	3	0
" charges on ores	2,020	10	8
" drawing, filling, and landing	2,734	5	3
" parochial rates and compensation for land destroyed	428	13	8
" carriage of ores, &c., and freights of materials	4,049	7	2
" counting-house expenses	167	2	1
" paid to sick labourers of both sexes, from the sick-club, when unable to work	721	19	5
" paid for medical attendance	321	12	0
" Stores	16,311	4	8
	£76,691	16	3

Under the head of Stores, the following articles may be considered as constituting the principal items, making the above sum of £16,311.4.8, viz:-

	Tons	Cwt.	Qrs.	£	s.	d.
Coals, including carriage, &c., to the mine	2,208	16	1	2,021	12	1
Iron, of various sizes and descriptions	148	18	2	1,500	0	10
Steel, ditto ditto	5	13	1	218	4	6
Patent flat and round ropes	32	1	2	1,201	2	2
Candles (7121 dozen lbs.)	33	3	0	2,155	18	10
Best Russia tallow	5	11	2	304	16	2
Gunpowder (86,100 lbs.)	38	8	3	1,658	0	0
45 hides of leather (2390 lbs.)	1	1	1	224	6	7
425 fathoms of patent iron chain	2	5	1	73	4	0
95 bags of nails of various descriptions	7	2	2	165	3	5
Foundry bills for castings, including a new steam-engine and weighing-bridge				2,150	8	2
57,759 feet of debenture timber (Dram and Longsound)				3,041	7	1
1044 ditto yellow and red pine				79	4	9
1232 ditto American oak				155	1	9
300,000 ditto patent safety fuze (12,500 coils)				472	17	11
1133 dozen pick and shovel hilts				115	8	11
1290 yards engine shag and poldavey				67	11	6
1356 gallons of cod-oil				197	4	4
221 ditto rape-oil				49	9	2
25 dozen of copper powder-cans				41	5	0
Sieves, riddles, and stamps grates				167	11	9
Account-books and stationery				36	0	10
Sundries, of various descriptions				222	4	11
				£16,311	4	8

The following is a Statistical Account of the Agents, Labourers, and others, employed in and on the foregoing Mine; exclusive of Carriers, and those casually employed, viz:-

Designation	Average Monthly No.	Wages £	s.	d.	Remarks
Agents, &c.	13	9	3	0	Agents, 7; Clerks, 5; Storekeeper, 1.
Engineers	1	8	8	0	
Mapper and Dialler	1	8	8	0	With occasional assistance from a Clerk.
Tributers	338	3	10	9	Less 2s. per month, viz.—1/3d.
Tut-workmen	360	2	19	9	for Sick Club; 3d. for Death
Sump-men	44	3	12	5	Fund; and 6d. for Medical Attendance.

Boys underground	15	0	17	6	Employed Blowing Air Machines.
Day Labourers ditto	140	2	12	0	Maximum, £3.5.0.; Minimum £1.19.0.
Day and Monthly Labourers at the surface	196	0	0	0	Including Smiths, Carpenters, Engine Men, Trammers, Dividers, &c., &c.
Boys employed at surface	302	1	0	7	Maximum £1.12.6.; Minimum 8/8d.
Women and Girls, ditto, ditto	324	0	16	3	Ditto, £1.3.10.; Ditto 8/8d.
Total Number employed	1734				

Dated 23rd March, 1839   Wм. Davis, Purser of the Mine.

(*NOTE:* The income for the Day and Monthly Labourers at the surface quoted as £0.0.0. is obviously a mis-print, their earnings in 1837 averaging £2.0.1. per month. It is worth noting the apparent substantial use of patent safety fuze which had been invented by William Bickford of Tuckingmill, Camborne some seven years previously. Prior to 1831 miners customarily used goose quills or straws filled with gunpowder to ignite the charge.[8] It would appear that Fowey Consols was in the forefront of the adoption of the new invention. In a lecture given by Sir Charles Lemon in 1838 on The Statistics of the Copper Mines of Cornwall[9] comparative figures were given between the materials used at the Consolidated Mines in Gwennap and Fowey Consols for the year of 1836. The two mines produced approximately one quarter of the copper ore mined in Cornwall at the time.

	Consolidated		*Fowey Consols*	
Tributers & Tutworkers	833		740	
Gunpowder (lbs) & cost	64,000	£1,408	66,500	£1,460
Cost of safety fuze		£262.10.0		£475.4.2

No figures were given for the actual length of fuze used, but on the assumption that the figures give a true and undistorted comparison between the two mines then the cost indicates that the usage of the new fuze at Fowey Consols was nearly twice that at the Consolidated Mines.

The lengthy dispute regarding the best way of working the Carruggatt sett was finally resolved in the early part of 1839. Richard Foster wanted the adit for the workings to be driven westwards into the sett from the valley situated to the east. This would have served a dual purpose, for as well as draining that part of the mine the ground would effectively be tried as the adit progressed, with the possibility of discovering promising lodes. This was unacceptable to Treffry because of the cost, which was estimated at more than £1000, and also because Foster had still not formally granted the sett of his land under which a large part of the adit was to pass. Of the four main adits at Fowey Consols at this time one was driven eastwards into the sett from Wheal Hope, passing under Tregaske's shaft and into Wheal Treasure. The other three adits were driven into the mine from the valley to the south, discharging into the stream which runs parallel to where the railway is today. One drained the Sawle's section of Lanescot, another about 1200 yards long passed under Hodge's, Sampson's and Union shafts before terminating at Austen's, and the easternmost adit commenced just to the east of Treesmill and originally drained the Wheal Fortune sett. It had been extended over the years, and ran north to Polsue's shaft and then west, passing under Ray's and on to Sampson's. A branch ran northwards from Ray's to Trathan's and towards John's shaft, and another branch ran from Polsue's shaft to Bottrall's with a junction to Pidler's. Treffry and Nicholas Kendall wanted to use an existing branch of the Wheal Fortune adit and drive north into Carruggatt from near John's shaft, and this scheme was eventually adopted. An idea of the time scale involved in constructing the adit can be gained from a letter sent to Rashleigh by Kendall in the previous year: "I should add that the adit in question is one that has been steadily driving during nearly 20 years, and for the last 15 years Carruggatt and Polharmon have been always in view."

In the early 1830's Treffry had started to acquire land to enable him to build a railway from the Par Canal basin through the Luxulyan Valley to Luxulyan, continuing onwards to Molinnis near Bugle. This railway would open up the china clay district and enable clay to be exported through Par Harbour. An early attempt to build the line was unsuccessful, the reasons given by Treffry being the hardness and difficulty of the ground in the valley and problems with the contractors. In October 1838 he had purchased the Manor

of Towan Blistra on the north Cornish coast, reputedly obtaining
it at a cheap price because he sent a poor man to bid for him at
the auction in Truro.[10] The manor contained the small fishing
village and harbour of Newquay, which gave Treffry the potentially
very valuable asset of a north Cornish port. The transport of copper
ore to South Wales from south Cornish ports and the return journey
laden with coal involved a long and hazardous journey around
Land's End, a voyage that could be avoided if the ships sailed from
north Cornwall. The building of the railway line was re-started and
to overcome the problems encountered in attempting to run the
line up through the Luxulyan Valley Treffry decided to extend the
canal to Ponts Mill and then build an incline from near the new
canal basin up the hillside on the eastern side of the valley to the
required height. This would allow the journey to take place through
to Molinnis without further severe gradients, with a proposed extension to Roche some two miles further on. This entailed crossing the
Luxulyan Valley by means of a viaduct where it curved north east,
and the foundation stone for the viaduct was laid in March 1839.
The fact that the valley was to be crossed at this point opened up
a new source of water for Fowey Consols mine from the north west
at Molinnis Moor, and the viaduct was built to incorporate a leat
to carry water as well as the railway across the valley. After it
crossed the valley the new leat ran parallel to the original Fowey
Consols leat but at a higher level, eventually joining it after the
new leat had operated a water wheel (30' x 8' 6") installed to haul
wagons up the new incline. The wheel pit was built to hold a wheel
up to 50' in diameter but the smaller wheel proved adequate for
haulage.[11] At the ceremony to lay the foundation stone of the
viaduct Sir John Colman Rashleigh stated: "I have little doubt that
he (Treffry) has it in contemplation to carry a line right across the
country to Newquay", and Treffry himself said that he had the
honour "of laying the foundation stone of a work which he hoped
would descend to posterity." It was estimated that the construction
would take two years,[12] and it was eventually opened in 1842.

The long delayed working of Carruggatt had been an ambition
of Treffry's for nearly twenty years, and although he only managed
to become a joint proprietor of the sett it looked, in 1840, as if it
was destined to live up to expectations. The adit driven north from
near John's shaft had met with success, and on 16th January Treffry
wrote to William Rashleigh to tell him "we have cut a very kindly

lode at Carruggatt with good spots of copper ore in it. At present to investigate it would impede our direct progress, but as soon as we get sufficient air to work it by the new shaft being down we shall make a trial of it.'' While Carruggatt shaft was being sunk the 80″ pumping engine ordered from Harveys for Henrietta's shaft was finally being erected. Unfortunately for Treffry the mine was encountering short term financial problems again, and there was a delay in paying the bill for the engine of £2,300 in the summer of 1840. In 1839 the adventurers had paid themselves dividends totalling £18,432, but this was not fully covered by profits and part was paid out of reserves.[13] With little money left for emergencies the mine was vulnerable to an unexpected fall off in income, and this happened in the early part of 1840. Figures for the calendar year are not available from the mine records, but copper statistics for the whole county were compiled annually for various publications, and ran from the 1st July each year to the end of the following June. The following figures illustrate the fall in Fowey Consols' output and proceeds:-

		Tons of ore	Proceeds[14]
Year ended	30.6.1839	15,197	£88,361
ˮ	30.6.1840	12,560	£68,662

Income increased in the next year however and this was only a temporary problem, which was just as well because the Devon & Cornwall Bank at St. Austell declined to lend him additional funds.[15] In a letter to the bank he detailed the costs of development work at the old Wheal Treasure sett at £3000, £5000 had been spent re-opening Lanescot and the cost of sinking Henrietta's shaft to the 110 fathom level and establishing communicating levels was given at £4000. It was estimated that this shaft would cut the main lode at 200 fathoms below the adit.

Treffry believed in protecting home industry, and during 1840 he was continuing an ultimately unsuccessful campaign to prevent the duties on imported copper ores being withdrawn. He was concerned that unhindered imports of rich copper ore would reduce the price of copper metal to such an extent that it would make the Cornish copper mining industry unprofitable, throwing thousands of miners out of work and causing massive distress. Britain was still the largest producer of copper ore in the world, and nearly all of it came from

Cornwall. Imported ore, mainly from Chile and Cuba, was increasing steadily and was running at about 42,000 tons in 1840,[16] but it was to be many years before the huge copper deposits in the New World were fully exploited. Treffry was opposed by many manufacturers and the Swansea copper smelting interests. He was subjected to personal and anonymous attacks through the columns of the Mining Journal by a correspondent who styled himself 'YZ'. In the edition of 29th August 1840 'YZ'[17] pointed out that for Fowey Consols "to raise 1,200 or 1,300 tons of ores a month, and to maintain that rate for years, requires a very great extent of ground to be opened, and constant discoveries to be made . . . It is very easy to profess great anxiety for the working miner, and to call for the prohibition of foreign ores; the title of the miners' friend may thus be earned cheaply by, what I must call, mere hypocritical whining; but the truth is, the profits kill the mine, and a few years of forced working to keep up a large dividend would do the poor miners more injury than all the foreign ores that ever were, or will be, imported." As part of a very lengthy reply Treffry stated "as to the insinuation, that through the greediness of pocketing profits, I would not only risk the destruction of Fowey Consols mine, but turn unemployed upon the wide world, probably in a state of destitution, miners and others who, by their earnings at that mine, maintain a population exceeding 7,000 souls, is no light charge – it is quite monstrous! . . . Where is the mine that during the last year expended in tutwork only upwards of £15,000, or where is the mine that has had so much work done in her during the last twenty years as Fowey Consols, which has still more unexplored maiden ground within her ambit than the whole extent of any mine in Cornwall, with machinery to keep her in fork (drained) for twenty years to come?"[18] On 1st April 1842 the West Briton reported a speech made by Treffry to underline the importance of a successful copper mining industry to the economy of Cornwall. He stated that the total amount of copper ore sold by Fowey Consols and its constituent mines from 1815 to the end of 1841 was 234,486 tons which sold for £1,422,633. The sale proceeds had been allocated as follows during that period:-

	£
Mineral dues paid to landowners	95,610
Compensation to farmers for damaged land	2,436
Parochial rates	8,883
Dividends to adventurers	173,913
Cash in the Reserve fund	6,082
Stores purchased	237,707
Estimated value of stock on the mine, engines and materials	60,000
Balance, being estimated amount paid in wages	838,002
	1,422,633

The Prime Minister, Sir Robert Peel, was about to bring in the first of his Free Trade budgets and Treffry was part of a group appointed from Cornwall to plead for the retention of copper tariffs. A young W. E. Gladstone was present at the meeting. The Cornish delegation was unsuccessful, Thomas Robins telling William Rashleigh "I hear Sir Robert Peel received the deputation from Cornwall very courteously but is not likely to give way to the representations made to him – I find that Mr. Treffry is in a great rage, but I think there are no grounds for much alarm about copper." The import tariffs on hundreds of items were either reduced or abolished by Peel in 1842, and for copper the tariff was reduced, only to be abolished altogether in 1848.

Notes
1. The engine was purchased by Thomas Wicksteed for the East London Waterworks Company at Old Ford, the contract for re-erecting it after repairs and alterations being given to Harveys and William West for £7,600. D. B. Barton: The Cornish Beam Engine, 1965.
2. Commenting on the Fowey Consols lodes in his book "A Treatise on Ore Deposits" published in 1896 J. A. Phillips stated: "The lodes in this locality are much contorted in length and depth, and are remarkable for the number of junctions they make with one another in their downward course."
3. WB 11.8.1837.
4. RCG 25.6.1847. The MJ carries correspondence suggesting that at this time smelters often recovered silver from ores without the knowledge of the Cornish mines from which they were purchased.
5. CN 2604 at the CRO.
6. Ken Brown carried out a comprehensive examination of the remains

of Davis's whim engine house before it was removed in 1994. He discovered that the engine beam and flywheel were entirely contained within the house, with the winding drum outside. It was therefore very similar in layout to the preserved whim engine at Levant mine near St. Just (built 1840 by Harveys), with a difference between the placement of the shaft, winding drum and engine cylinder. At Levant the arrangement is shaft-cylinder-drum, and at Davis's and Powne's engines at Fowey Consols it is shaft-drum-cylinder. Treffry had the chance to buy Levant in its early days (letter 23.10.1824, TF 916 at the CRO), and his failure to do so deprived him of an interest in one of Cornwall's most successful tin and copper mines which operated until October 1930.

7. Lean's Engine Reporter, May 1837.
8. B. Earl: Cornish Explosives, 1978.
9. R. Burt: Cornish Mining, 1969.
10. MJ 15.7.1882.
11. WB 2.2.1844.
12. WB 15.3.1839.
13. TF 932 at the CRO and MJ 5.9.1840.
14. MJ 29.8.1840.
15. The first Minute Book of the Devon and Cornwall Bank has survived and is held in the archives of Lloyds Bank. In September 1840 the General Manager of the bank met Treffry at St. Austell and "expressed to him the wishes of the Directors that his debt should be considerably reduced and he had stated his willingness to meet their wishes."
16. MJ 24.7.1847. Slavery was used to produce some foreign ore: "Let due protection be given to the British miner against the ores raised by slaves in Cuba." RCG 1.4.1842.
17. In this edition of the MJ a correspondent suggested that 'YZ' was Sir Hussey Vivian. He was referring to Sir Richard Hussey Vivian, the eldest son of the copper smelter John Vivian. Sir Richard was a partner in the family firm and he had a distinguished military career, commanding part of the cavalry reserve of Wellington's army at the Battle of Waterloo and leading the last cavalry charge against the retreating French army as it was finally driven from the field. He had been a Member of Parliament for both Windsor & Truro before representing Bodmin from 1837 until his death in 1842, becoming Baron Vivian of Glynn in 1841 and the first Lord Vivian. His nephew, Henry Hussey Vivian, was born in 1821 and eventually headed the family company, becoming the first Lord Swansea in 1893. Other letters appeared in the MJ in 1847 under the nom-de-plume 'YZ'.
18. MJ 5.9.1840.

CHAPTER V

THE 1842 PARLIAMENTARY COMMISSION

IN THE spring of 1841 Fowey Consols was visited by a Parliamentary Commission set up to report on the employment of children in the mines of Cornwall and Devon.[1] The Commission was headed by Charles F. Barham (1804–84), Senior Physician at the Royal Cornwall Infirmary, Truro and a pioneer in the study of miners' diseases. Barham became Mayor of Truro in 1857, President of the Royal Institution of Cornwall from 1859 to 1861 and the Barham Memorial Wing at the Royal Institution is named after him.

The Commission's Report, published in 1842, gives a unique insight into the working lives of the hundreds of men, women and children who were employed at the mine. For the surface workers the morning journey to work had to be started early to arrive at the mine at 7 a.m. in the summer and by daybreak in the winter. In relative terms the mine offered shorter working hours and better pay than other, agriculturally-based, jobs in the district and it attracted labourers from a wide area. In the early days long distances were walked to work, but in later years people settled nearer to the mine. In 1841 some were still travelling up to five miles in each direction every day,[2] but most lived within one or two miles.[3]

The dressing of the copper ore at surface to separate it from the waste materials found in the lode was very labour intensive. The large lumps of lode material were first broken down into smaller pieces or ragged by men using 12lb.[4] hammers and similarly spalled by women using lighter hammers of 3 lbs. The ores were then taken to the picking sheds which mainly ran north-south at Fowey Consols, almost certainly to facilitate the flow of water down the slope and through the sheds in a trough. After washing in the trough the ore was placed on a long central table in front of young girls who picked or sorted the ores. The better quality ore was then

Ragging

Spalling

Cobbing

Contemporary sketches showing ragging, spalling & cobbing.
From J. Henderson, on the methods generally adopted in Cornwall in Dressing
Tin and Copper Ores, Proceedings of the Institution of Civil Engineers (1857-58)

taken to the cobbing houses where women and girls sat in a long row breaking it into pieces about the size of a chestnut. They used a small anvil by their side and a hammer, sometimes with a small wooden screen to stop their legs being covered by the cobbed ore. We know from accounts of other copper mines that cobbing houses could be intimidating places. In the great cobbing house at Dolcoath, known as 'The Roarer',[5] 60 women sat in a row and it was said that it was a place where no youth dare show his face. Dr. Barham commented on the dress of the women employed in the mines[6]: "The occupations of the females not being usually very dirty, the ordinary dress, or one only slightly varied, is worn at the mine; additional protection is, however, commonly given to the lower part of the legs by wrapping them in woollen bands in the winter and often in cotton ones in the summer. A certain smartness is noticeable in the bonnets, and in the manner of wearing them; they are generally small in the winter, and thrown rather back on the head, chiefly made of some lively-coloured material in some districts and of straw in others; whilst in summer they are commonly large, straight, and projecting, with a long loose border, such as may afford effectual shelter from the sun", Having commented on "a passion for dress, as very extensively diffused among the young women connected with the mines in every district", he continued: "As a medical man, he has often had cases brought under his notice in which he has been satisfied that disordered health has been mainly induced by coarse and scanty nourishment, whilst the patients have presented themselves in dresses only to be procured at very considerable cost . . . there is reason to believe that the provision of warm inner garments for the colder season is by no means correspondent with the outlay on those external ones which may serve to increase the personal attraction of the wearers . . . the younger girls are neither equally well clothed, nor equally clean; and the work of the greater number (picking) exposes them more to wet and dirt. Still there is generally, even here, a degree of neatness proving the disposition to do as well as circumstances permit." One of the Fowey Consols surgeons, W. W. Tayler, wrote in 1851[7] "the bal maidens carry their fondness for dress to extremes; all the dresses exhibited in the plates of the monthly books of fashion may be seen at Tywardreath or St. Blazey on a fine Sunday afternoon, not even omitting the additional accompaniments of parasols, lace edged pocket handkerchiefs, etc. However, the money

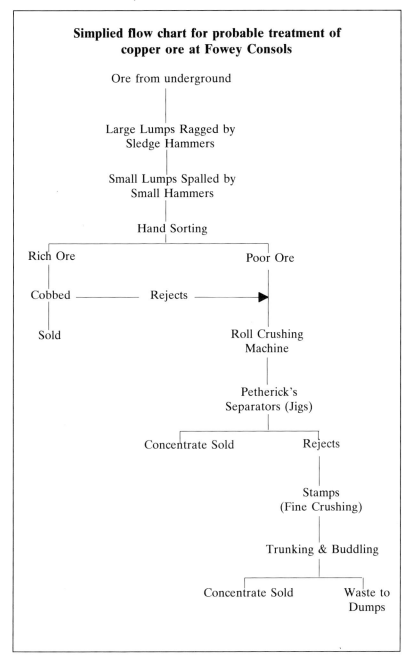

Simplied flow chart for probable treatment of copper ore at Fowey Consols

Ore from underground

Large Lumps Ragged by
Sledge Hammers

Small Lumps Spalled by
Small Hammers

Hand Sorting

Rich Ore   Poor Ore

Cobbed ———————— Rejects ————————▶

Sold   Roll Crushing
                                 Machine

                                 Petherick's
                                 Separators (Jigs)

        Concentrate Sold   Rejects

                                 Stamps
                                 (Fine Crushing)

                                 Trunking & Buddling

        Concentrate Sold   Waste to
                                      Dumps

that produces all this finery has been hardly earned; and if the individual prefers that mode of gratifying her feelings, who has the right to sneer at it?"

In the next stage of ore dressing the poorer quality ores were reduced further in size by being put through the roll crushing machines[8] and then taken to Petherick's separators to recover finer sized copper ore. Some lower quality material was put through the stamps and concentrated for sale by boys using water processing to carry off the waste. This finely ground material called slimes was run suspended in water through pits dug in the ground (trunking and buddling), where the more valuable ore particles with a higher specific gravity settled nearest the end where the water flowed in to the pit. Barham wrote: "The work of a large proportion of the boys employed at the surface exposes them to wet and dirt; and, however wet or dirty they may be, the same clothes are worn from the time they rise in the morning until bed-time at night." Having commented on the fact that thick woollen frocks (smocks?) gave them good protection against the elements and that they made some effort to clean themselves after work he said "more might certainly be done in respect of both person and clothing, still it is exceedingly rare to meet with an example of squalid filthiness in any member of a miner's family."

The dinner break at the mine started at 12.00 and lasted for half an hour in winter and up to one hour in the summer. The surface workers ate wherever they chose in the warmer months and in the winter a building was provided, warmed by a long iron cylinder passing through it, heated by a fire at one end. The tube was also used to warm food, and ovens were kept in several buildings throughout the mine where pasties could be warmed at a charge of 1d. per week. According to the 1842 report "there is little or no mixing of the sexes at their meal. The younger boys very often eat their pasties almost by snatches, and make the most of the time at some game. Preparatory washing or changing of dress is seldom practised. There is no work going on during the time allowed for dinner which requires the attention of the young people. The shortness of the time is complained of, by the females especially, where they are limited to half an hour."

Work at the mine finished for surface workers at dusk in the winter and between 5 and 6 p.m. in the summer. Much of this work was done at piece rates where there was a direct relationship between the output achieved and pay received. Specific tasks were often set after which the boy or girl was allowed to leave the mine early. Unless tending machinery there was no work done on Sundays, and the only general holidays were Christmas Day and Good Friday. Work usually finished about one hour early on Saturdays, and little work was done after lunch on pay days. For the miners pay and setting day at Fowey Consols took place on the third Saturday in each month, and the surface workers were paid on the fourth Saturday.[9] With the very large number of people employed at the mine's peak pay day was a major exercise, and to reduce the time taken one person usually collected the money on behalf of several colleagues: "Much care is now generally taken to pay them with such a proportion of silver as may enable them to make the division without having recourse to the shop or public-house for change." It is also probable that some of the surface workers were in partnership with one another, the leader collecting the pay. The 1842 report gives a sample of the wages of some of those employed at dressing the copper ore on the mine "taken promiscuously from the Cost Book for one year to end of March 1841." Jane Bartle and Jane Hooper received 4d. per day with an average monthly wage of 4/11d. Catherine Cotty earned 11d. per day and averaged £1.3.0. per month, whilst H. Carpenter did rather better with a monthly average of £1.7.4 in tending a jigging machine (separator). The annual report of the mine for 1838 gives the average wage for boys at surface of £1.0.7 per month (Max. £1.12.6, min. 8/8d.) and for women and girls the figure was 16/3d. (Max. £1.3.10, min. 8/8d.). The number of young people employed on the mine at this time was given as follows:-[10]

Age	Girls	Boys Underground	At surface
8–9			3
9–10			11
10–11			23
11–12	8	1	6
12–13	15	3	42
13–14	21	2	38
14–15	24	3	33
15–16	15	7	21
16–17	15	13	13
17–18	18	8	6

It was quite normal to take on additional girls twice a month to assist at sampling, when they would be required to work late into the evening. The ores were sampled by prospective purchasers prior to sale, and the report states "The division of the ores into separate parcels presents some peculiarities in the labour of the females, and constitutes an animated scene in the larger mines. The general heap, containing, perhaps, some hundred tons, is surrounded by a number of pairs of girls with hand-barrows, which are filled from the edge of the heap by a party stationed round, in a regular succession, dictated by a girl appointed to the post. The barrows are then carried off rapidly, and emptied as the germs of a certain number of distinct parcels; and to each of these a barrowful is added in regular order, so that the total number in every one is the same. This business is attended with some bustle and hilarity. Those who fill the barrows exchange places after a time with those who carry them." Following the completion of the Par Canal the ores were taken to Par Harbour for sampling.

Children were, by the standards of the day, kindly treated. Discipline on the mine was exercised with a light hand, and spaleing (a fine) was sometimes used as a punishment. William Davis did refer in the report to the fact that "many years since corporal punishment was inflicted here on two boys for theft, by order of the county magistrates; and three or four instances have occurred of fathers correcting their children publicly, in front of the counting house, and in the presence of the agents, having their election either to correct their sons or have them discharged from the mine." Dr. Barham found that "The external appearance of the children and young persons employed at the surface, taken as a class, is that of robust health. The complexion is generally florid, the person well formed, the expression alert and cheerful. Among the girls as they approach towards womanhood there is an inclination towards embonpoint (stoutness), and many of them possess a considerable share of personal beauty; . . . the greater part of the boys are drafted off to underground work before the frame is at all fully developed, but they are generally healthy and well formed as long as they continue at the surface. The abundant supply of fresh air, and the variety of muscular movement, are the main causes of their healthiness and their freedom from deformity respectively" and "even when labour is prolonged, it is rare to perceive any external sign that the flow of youthful spirits has been dried up."

Women were never employed underground in Cornish mines. The prospect of higher pay and shorter working hours was a great incentive for the boys to go underground at the earliest opportunity. Barham wrote: "After the age of 14, a boy who has worked underground would be very reluctant to return to surface labour". William Pace, chief surgeon at Fowey Consols, commented on the care of children underground: "The miners have very strict injunctions from our agents and captains to take the greatest care of them, and they are not allowed to descend or ascend without being preceded by a miner, until they have been at work for a considerable period, and are considered capable to take care of themselves." Dressed in their flannel shirt and trousers, stout shoes and hard hat the boys entered a dark and dangerous world, illuminated only with a tallow candle attached to their hat with sticky clay. They usually started underground by either working the duck (ventilation) machines, hauling tackle or wheeling barrows. The duck machine was "a sort of hydraulic bellows, consisting of two boxes or cisterns, one moving inverted within the other, which is filled with water. The moving power is applied at the end of a lever, very much like the handle of a common pump, and by raising the inner cistern, the impure air is drawn in, to be expelled from its upper part when depressed, by a proper arrangement of valves and pipes." Hauling tackle was the use of a windlass to raise materials and rock up through winzes and "a good deal of labour is involved in this occupation, but the air is not usually very impure in the upper level in which the windlass is placed." Wheeling barrows was "always laborious" and "the boys are often allowed to leave, at the end of six hours barrow-work, where it is continuous, that period being considered equivalent to eight hours of other labour: if the stuff has been cleared away, they are not even detained so long." When considered big and strong enough the boys would be taken into "concern" (partnership) to start their employment as tributers and tutworkers, sharing in the risks and profits of their companions: "It may be confidently stated, that no hiring of children or young persons takes place in the mines of the west of England to which they are not voluntary parties . . . there is a very general consideration on the part of the men of the age and powers of their young fellow labourers, and a disposition to relieve them from any excess of toil, even at the expense of increased exertion of their own. The very frequent association in work of children with their parents or near relatives contributes to the promotion of this generous and manly feeling."

Life underground was extemely hard. Fowey Consols used the traditional eight hour cores or shifts starting at 6 a.m., 2 p.m. and 10 p.m. with the men taking turns so that an equal amount of night work was undertaken by each. When necessary a double core or stem would be worked, usually when a favourable tribute contract was about to run out, or when a miner stood in for a sick colleague to prevent him losing his contract. The maximum depth from surface in 1841 was approximately 220 fathoms, and the lodes in the mine varied in thickness from a few inches to eight feet. As the mine became deeper it was difficult to ventilate the bottom levels which, in places, were very hot with temperatures recorded of up to 88°F (31°C). In coal mines ventilation had to be adequate to combat the risk of gas or dust explosions, but this was not a requirement in metal mines and the long term medical effects of working in poor air were not fully acknowledged in 1842. The usual underground levels at Fowey Consols were 6' high and 4' wide, but where air had to be piped in the height was 7'. The use of duck machines was one method of circulating air underground, and after 1840 air pumps were installed in Austen's shaft.[11] Here the piston of the pump which forced the air into the ventilation pipes was operated either by the engine beam or pump rod as it rose and fell. Air was taken in to some levels merely by allowing water to flow into a funnel and down a pipe, taking fresh air with it.

The wages received for working underground at this time are found in evidence given by Davis to the 1842 Commission: "I may state that our tutworkers wages have averaged nearly £3 per month for some years past, and with this some men of frugal habits appear to live comfortably, and rear a numerous family without in any way becoming a burthen to their parishes; whilst the tributers, whose wages generally average from 10/- to 15/- per month more than the tutworkmen (though sometimes for months together their wages may be very low), are for the most part in debt, and some to a considerable extent, where they have not been so fortunate for a long time as to have what the miners call a sturt (an unusually profitable contract) to liquidate them from their pecuniary diffi- culties." Both classes of miner paid 1/3d. for the sick club, 3d. to the death fund and 6d. for medical attendance each month. They received the following benefits detailed in the 1838 mine report:

"Each miner in this mine receives £1.10.0. per month during illness, and whilst unable to follow his usual avocation (occupation) has medical attendance with medicine provided for himself, and such branches of his family as may be dependant on him for support; together with an allowance of £5, to his family or representatives, in a case of death, to provide for funeral expenses etc." The women and girls received 12/- per month when sick for a deduction of 1d. from every 5/- of their wages up to a monthly maximum contribution of 5d.

The 1842 Report stated that the surface operations in mines "are very free from occasions of accident; and such as do occur are for the most part slight, arising from strains or falls, or casual blows with the tools." In comparison with the frequent accidents underground no doubt surface accidents were rare, but this would have been little consolation to those who were unfortunate enough to be entangled and mangled in poorly protected surface machinery. One such event at Fowey Consols in December 1842 was referred to in a letter to William Rashleigh from W. E. Geach, his Land Agent: "A poor girl got her clothes entangled in the wheels of the separating machine, which revolves at a rapid rate; she was instantly drawn between the cogs and whirled around at a frightful rate till both her legs were so mangled as to pass between the wheels without any further impression being made on them. She was carried home and a surgeon was quickly on the spot. She still survives although but little hope remains of her recovery." The letter was written approximately one week after the accident, and the horrors of suffering a major accident and the medical skills needed to treat a badly injured patient with the minimal resources available were detailed by William Pace in the 1842 Report. He gave examples of nine very serious but non fatal accidents which took place underground over an unspecified period of time. The following report was given on Jacob Waters, a miner 46 years old – "Had a fall underground with a piece of timber. I saw him immediately after his comrades had carried him home, and had him undressed and put into bed. On examination I found a very severe compound fracture of the tibia and fibula of the right leg, the tibia protruding several inches, with such extensive laceration of the muscles of the limb, that it might have been twisted off very easily. After cleaning the wound, (I beg to observe here, that the wounds of miners received under ground require the greatest care and attention on the part of the surgeon to remove if possible every particle of dirt or mundic from them; if this be not particularly attended to, very severe constitutional derangement is the consequence, attended with considerable danger to the patient,) and gentle extension being made, I reduced the fractures and placed the lacerated portions of the muscles, &c., in their natural position, as far as the case could permit of. The man suffered great pain and uneasiness in the limb, and in a few weeks I removed a partially exfoliated portion of the tibia. I was frequently urged by the man himself to amputate the limb, but declined doing so, as I always have done, and shall do, if I see a chance of saving a limb without risking the patient's life. Batley's Sedative Solution was frequently given, and the man's strength kept up by a generous and nutritious diet, aided by quinine, porter, wine, &c. This case was to me a most anxious one, – one which required a vast deal of watching, care, and attendance on my part, and great patience on the part of the patient himself; but it gives me great pleasure to be able to say, that in about eighteen months from the period of the accident the man was capable of renewing his labour under ground, with a perfectly straight and strong limb."

The two surgeons, Pace and Tayler, were long time observers of the men who worked at Fowey Consols and they have given us an account of the lives the miners led. An evidently frustrated Willliam Pace told the Commission "my observations have led me to conclude that if a miner were to take care of his health, and have timely medical assistance, and adhere to the advice given to him, that his age would equal that of any other labourer; but a miner's mode of living is bad, and I believe many a good constitution is thrown away by bad management. For instance, miners at a very early age (14 or 16) contract a habit of smoking tobacco, and unfortunately it increases to such an excess, that I am inclined to believe that more constitutions are ruined by that and drinking, than by their labour. I have felt much interested in the welfare of the miners, and having had such a multitude of them under my charge for several years, I have taken many and frequent opportunities of counselling them on the management of their health; but in very many instances I am sorry to say that my advice has been mocked at, and my time wasted; this I attribute to their being generally uninstructed, nevertheless it has not, nor will it prevent me from doing what I deem incumbent on me. When once the habit of smoking is contracted, I have before observed that it increases rapidly. The moment a miner wakes in the morning, the first thing he does is to strike a light and smoke his pipe; then he makes his fire and boils the water for his breakfast, by that time his pipe is finished; and as soon as he has taken his breakfast he fills another pipe and smokes that on his way to the mine; as soon as he gets underground perhaps he smokes another, and so he continues to smoke all day; if he happens to wake during the night he will have a pipe, and at the end of the week it is not unusual for him to have smoked a quarter of a pound of tobacco or more; the consequence is, that it takes away his appetite, after a time destroys the digestive powers, tremors follow, and the miner becomes blanched and emaciated. Next, to his mode of living: – a miner rarely eats anything but cold potato pasties, with perhaps a small quantity of salted pork baked in them; and frequently the pasty he has taken to the mine with him to eat in the course of the day will be taken back with him at night untouched, because he has no appetite to eat it; and so, literally speaking, time after time, the system has no nourishment afforded it, and is still continued to be drained by a constant discharge of saliva, caused by the excessive use of tobacco. I have mentioned before, with regard to drinking, a miner after working hard will frequently, in his way home, go into the first beer-shop he comes to and drink a pint of beer or porter, because he will tell you he feels weak, and it will give him an appetite for his supper; after he has had one pint he will have a second and a third, and I have known when two or three of them have met together that they drank two or three gallons; this frequently happens on the day they receive their pay. Others again I have known to drink half a pint of brandy and eat half a pound of cheese at one time: all these inconsistent excesses must of course tend to weaken and disorganise the system. I have often cautioned the miners against a very dangerous custom, and advised them to discontinue it; and that is, as soon as they arrive at the surface, after working perhaps nearly naked, they will plunge their feet immediately into the cold waters in the leats or drains, and frequently wash the breast with it whilst the perspiration is running down it in globules. Again, miners will climb too rapidly, there is no necessity for it, they are not obliged to be on the surface at a certain time or moment, or to descend within a given time, so long as they work the number of hours allotted to each core, therefore the mischief that it produces is brought on voluntarily; they are equally as incautious underground, for they will sit upon cold stones and stand in the cross-cuts after working hard, and whilst in a copious perspiration, frequently will drink a gallon of cold water in less than six hours. When they meet with foul air, and feel it to affect them, they are as negligent as ever, and delay applying for medical treatment until they can work no longer. The symptoms they mostly complain of after working in it, is a general lassitude, with pain and aching about the knees, calves of the legs, pain in the head, tickling cough, load on the chest, dim sight, fluttering about and palpitation of the heart, confined bowels, and a black sooty expectoration, and in some habits where the system has been previously impaired the absorbents have been considerably affected, and a complete and sudden oedematous* attack produced.

I have had opportunities of observing, in a few cases, that agricultural labourers who have abandoned their employment and become miners are perfectly unfit for underground work, and very soon become affected, and have been obliged to return to their former employ; but miners who have through the whole course of their lives been accustomed, and from boyhood habituated, to work underground, and have taken care of themselves and not indulged in the baneful excesses I have alluded to, I have no hesitation in saying that I believe the periods of their lives would equal those of any other labourers."

William Tayler found the miners to be industrious and wrote in 1851: "many of them may be seen, after returning from their set hours of work, often after toiling all night, labouring diligently in their garden or potato ground. Indeed, the miner is rarely idle: on a wet day, when precluded from out-door work, he occupies the time in mending the children's shoes, or in some of the mechanical contrivances in which miners greatly excel. They take a great deal of pride in their gardens, which are no less remarkable for their neatness, than for the beauty and quality of their flowers and vegetables, often being able to compete successfully with the horticultural productions of the gentry in the neighbourhood, as the various exhibitions and gardening societies annually testify. He may also be termed a provident man, two out of three being voluntary

*A build-up of fluids in the body.

members of some benefit society, paying from 14/- to 16/- a year, in addition to what may be termed the compulsory payments to the mine-club, so that in sickness, unless under peculiar circumstances, he is not necessitated to apply for parochial relief." Of the bal maidens he said "I may observe they are strong, healthy, active, well-formed girls, and make, for the most part, very good wives, generally contriving to hold the reins of power in their own hands, ruling their husbands and finances with a good deal of tact and discretion: for be it known, that the whole of the earnings or gettings are generally entrusted to the wife's care; and, like a good Chancellor of the Exchequer, she lays out the surplus to the best possible advantage."[12]

In April 1841 some of Mr. Hennah's boys and girls were interviewed for the 1842 Commission. The father of one boy gave additional evidence. Their uncomplicated and open testimony is a reminder of working conditions for the majority of the men, women and children who worked at Fowey Consols mine.

Jacob Waters, 17 years and 10 months old
Is employed at the 67-fathom level, beating the borer and turning it. Has been 16 months underground steadily. Before that worked underground for a very short time, when he was between 15 and 16. The air is poor where he is now. He has been there about four months, driving a level. He feels a pain in the head after working some time, which lasts for some hours after he is come to the surface. Almost every morning he has a cough, and brings up some stuff as black as ink. Sometimes he feels a pain in the breast. He is employed at tutwork. They work regularly eight-hour cores; always from six a.m. to two p.m. They "shoot" (blast) three or four times a day, after which they cannot go into the end for half an hour, as it is full of smoke. He then eats his pasty in the level, where there is better air. He went to work at "grass" at 12 years old. Worked two years at "jigging," and before that at the stamps. He can do his work very well. He does nothing after he comes up from under-ground. He cannot generally get water underground. Sometimes it is brought to the same level. He sweats a great deal and is very thirsty. When he worked at night, he only worked double stem once. He worked double stem yesterday, – from 6 a.m. to 11 p.m., coming up in the meantime for an hour. He changes in a cold place. There is no warm water. In winter-time the shoes are sometimes frozen

up in the chest. Has known several accidents happen to boys underground – some from falling away. His father was a miner, and had his leg broken by a piece of timber falling on him in the shaft. He went to day-school till he was 12, and afterwards to Sunday-school for a year and a half. He has since gone to an evening-school, where he learnt ciphering as far as compound division. The charge was 3d. a week if a candle was brought by the boy, and 3½d. otherwise.

Reads well, and can write.

William Blewett, 16 years and 4 months old
Works at the 55-fathom level. He went underground first about nine years of age. He then worked a month or two at a time, blowing air. The deepest place he was then in was the 150-fathom level. Afterwards, at 11, he worked for a year at a time. At less than 12 years of age he was taken into concern with his father; was employed beating the borer, &c. He took his night "core" regularly then. He worked in "poor air" for nine months before the last two months. He felt noises in the head, and his legs would feel so weak that he was forced to stop at every ladder. Was very much affected with cough when working in the "poor air," and would bring up black stuff. When a little boy, he felt but little inconvenience when blowing air; but sometimes found the air so bad that he would be sick at the same time. At present he never works double stem; nor after 12 at night; except the other night when waiting on the trammer. He went to school for a twelvemonth before he came to work at surface, which he did at seven years of age. Since that has gone, till lately, to Tywardreath Sunday-school. They are very seldom asked questions on what they read. He can write very little. Never did any ciphering.

Reads pretty well.

James Collins, 14 years and 5 months old
Has been underground about seven months. Was before about three years "to grass." He works now at the 80-fathom level, at the blowing-machine. Finds it rather hard work. When he goes into the end, when they want him, "his head aches from the poor air, after he comes out." Does not get sick, but cannot eat his meat there. Very seldom eats the pasty he takes underground, but eats his meal heartily at home after he comes up. Can hardly climb sometimes

from weakness in the legs. They carry water down themselves. Nobody is employed in this mine to carry water underground. He did not suffer "at grass" except sometimes from cold or getting wet, when "buddling." He is better now than when he went underground. Can eat his meat better. He is not in much smoke, and does not cough up the black sputa. He went to day-school "to a lot of places" before he came to the mine. Learnt nothing but reading. Has nearly forgotten what he learnt. Has not been to Sunday-school these nine months, for want of clothes. His father was a miner. "He went underground and took pain in his bowels, and died." This was nine years ago. His mother was left with four children. They are all employed at the mine. They can read. He worked last week three double stems, to keep the place for a comrade who met with an accident. "His candle went out, and he walked right into a winze." Once this week he has worked double stem for himself. He takes the night core with the men. He likes working underground better than "at grass," because the time is shorter. After he gets home he fetches water, works in the garden and so forth.

He has quite forgotten his reading, even in the Bible. Is hoarse, and says he has been so ever since he went underground.

John Rundle, 14 years old
Has been two years underground; works now at the 120-fathom level; he worked "to grass" before, for about three years and a half; his employment now is at the blowing-machine, and "haling tackle." The air is very bad; he cannot eat his pasty much; "he feels in his stomach all urging;" was well when at grass, except colds; worked then at "buddling," and "trunking;" was often wet; got his things dried at night when he went to bed; he finds it hard to climb the ladders; "likes underground better than to grass;" takes his night core in regular succession. His father is dead: "he was hurted," and went to work too soon afterwards; he left four children; one sister is married, and his two brothers work here. He went to day-school for three years and a half; learned to write pretty well, but has forgotten it since; goes to the Methodist Sunday-school; learns nothing but reading and spelling.

Reads badly.

Sketch of boy attending a jigging machine. He sits by the side of the hopper which is used to fill the sieves with copper ore to be dressed (processed).
The water reservoir is shown under the platform on which he sits. See page 40 for a description of the working cycle. The illustration is taken from The Saturday Magazine of 1st February 1834.

William Cullis, 17 years old.
Is employed "jigging" at the floors; he worked before at the "crushers" (grinder) but found it disagreed with his stomach; he was laid up three times; found his breathing short; lost his appetite, and brought up "old black trade", hears other boys complain of this sometimes; he has been five years at the mine; was three years at the jigging-machine; found his back ached sometimes; when at the grinder he used to work sometimes (four times in six months) day and night, from seven in the evening to five next morning; he has been healthy at the other work. He went to day-school for two years; learnt to write a little, but has forgotten it. He went to Sunday-school, Tywardreath Church- school, till about a year ago; only learnt reading and spelling.
Reads pretty well.

John Tillum, 14 years and 5 months old
Has worked underground most of his time for about four years past; works at the 170-fathom level, at the blowing-machine; it is very hot in the place; he can eat his pasty there; is hoarse now, has been so about three weeks; he very seldom works double stem. His father is a miner; has five children, all younger than himself. He went to day-school; learnt a little ciphering, which he has forgotten; can write a little. Goes to Sunday-school (Methodist) still; they only learn reading and spelling.
He reads pretty well.

John Spargoe, 11 years and 4 months old
Has been two years at the mine; is employed "jigging;" finds his back aches a little, but can play about afterwards; has a task once or twice a week, and can get away at two or three o'clock; works for himself afterwards when he can; never works at night. He went to day-school about a year before he came here; can read the Testament; goes to Sunday-school.
Reads badly. A healthy boy.

Mary Buller, 15 years and 10 months old
Has been working here about six years; generally "spalling" and "cobbing;" has generally had pretty good health; does not feel the work; leaves at five in the evening, never stays later, except once last month; perhaps once a week has a task, and can get away at

three or half-past three. "Most of the girls whom I know of, and I know a pretty deal of them in the mine, are strong and hearty." One of them (whose name she mentioned) "is terrible weakly, and looks very earthy, though she is 18". She went to day-school for three years, and learnt to read, and sew, and knit; has forgotten her reading; has not had clothes to go to Sunday-school; her mother is a widow, and could not afford to keep them at school.

Caroline Coom, 11 years old

Has been working here about two years; is employed "picking;" finds it easy and pleasant work; does not feel tired at the end of the day; none of the girls picking complain of anything; they get colds sometimes; she has no task; does not leave before five; has had a fever since she has been working at the mine; does not know how long ago. She goes to Sunday-school; reads the Testament there.

Reads a little.

Absalom George, 13 years old

He has worked underground about 13 months; is at the 45-fathom level; goes with his father instead of a man; gets wages as "part of a man;" he worked "to grass" for two years before. He went underground some time ago, and "blowed the machine" for about a fortnight; "the air was rather dead, and I was laid up, and was turned out from there." He mostly spits up, when he comes up from work, "nasty black trade;" he brings up some borers and other weights sometimes, "which makes him pant a good deal." Does not work at night, nor double stem; he likes it better than to grass, because the days are shorter, but he works hard when he gets home, and would be obliged to do so if at grass. His father has a little farm; he has seven children; two of them are younger than himself, and do nothing; the rest are employed. He went to day-school from about six years old, and about 10 "went to ball" (the mine). He learnt to write a little; can write his name. Goes to Sunday-school; can read pretty well.

John Penhall, 50 years old

Has been a miner from a boy; went underground at 15 or 16; has nine children, whom he has had taught to read and write; he has paid 5s. 6d. a quarter for the day-school, and 3d. a week for the evening-school; this is only open in the winter months. One of his boys he took underground at Fowey Consols about Christmas; he was 12 years old, a very fine and strong boy of his age. In about five weeks afterwards his boy was taken home on a shutter, with a broken leg and collar-bone; he fell off the ladder; could give no account of his fall, was not carrying anything; he was working himself in a distant part of the mine at the time. "When I was told what had happened, I travelled as fast as I could to the place; and I seemed to see, every few fathoms as I went, the body of my poor boy all crushed together: it was so clear that I stopped and rubbed my eyes, and asked myself whether I was in my right mind or no. When I got to the place, the boy was sitting upon a man's knee, looking up quite cheerful, only crying a little." He has found, when working in "poor air," that the pain in the forehead would often be very severe, and it was aggravated to an intense degree on stooping; so that he would dread to stoop to pick up a tool if he let one fall. The changes from heat to cold were at times very sudden; he might be working at a place, to get at which he would be obliged to wade for a considerable distance up to his breast in cold water; at other times he might work in a very hot place, from which they were obliged to retreat very frequently, as the water gained upon them, into the level, where they would all get huddled together as closely as possible, "creaming with cold;" then, when "the water was in fork" (removed), they would go in again, and drive at their work as hard as they could.

Notes
1. The Factory Act of 1833 had limited the working hours of children employed in the booming textile mills of the north, and attention was switched to mining. The Mines Act of 1842 subsequently forbade the employment underground of all women, and boys under 10 years of age.
2. Royal Cornwall Polytechnic Society Report 1841.
3. The population statistics for the parishes in this part of Cornwall indicate the impact of mining and related industrial growth, and its eventual decline. The figures are taken from an unpublished draft of the Victoria County Social & Economic History of Cornwall held at the Royal Institution of Cornwall.

	1811	1821	1831	1841	1851	1861	1871	1881
St. Blazey	442	938	2155	3234	3570	4224	3150	2762
Tywardreath	741	1238	2288	3152	3287	3379	2370	2129
Lanlivery	965	1318	1687	1809	1716	1657	1493	1388
Lostwithiel	825	933	1074	1186	1053	1017	922	931
Luxulyan	1047	1276	1288	1512	1439	1329	124	1098
Fowey	1319	1455	1767	1643	1606	1429	1394	1656
St. Sampson (Golant)	186	248	314	311	335	311	295	238
St. Austell	3686	6175	8758	10320	10750	11893	11793	11286

4. F. B. Michell: Ore Dressing in Cornwall, Journal of the Trevithick Society, No. 6 (1978).
5. John Corin: Trevithick Society Newsletter, No. 75.
6. The 1842 Parliamentary Commission covered the working practices of several Cornish mines without always specifically mentioning Fowey Consols. However Fowey Consols was one of the main mines examined for the report and there is sufficient additional evidence to confirm that the mine adopted the common working methods of the time.
7. RCG 18.4.1851.
8. The mechanical crusher or grinder had been invented in the early years of the century and was rather like a large mangle. Ore to be processed was fed from above between two iron cylinders, one of which revolved. The pulverised ore fell into sieves, and that which was still too coarse was put through the process again. The crushers were powered by water wheels, and the first machine at the mine was probably installed in the 1820s.
9. TF 3397 at the CRO.
10. William Davis commented on these figures: "I have not a doubt, from the great reluctance displayed amongst the youths in getting their names registered, and answering the several queries, (that they are) under an impression that a war is about to take place, and that this step is preparatory to their being called upon to go as soldiers as they term it, (and) that many at present working underground are returned amongst the adults, though under 18 years of age."
11. Lean's Engine Reporter April 1840, March 1843 and July 1845.
12. RCG 18.4.1851.

CHAPTER VI

'A GENERAL CALAMITY'

The increasing importance of the eastern part of the mine led to the building of a changing house and dry near Bottrall's shaft, and these would appear to date from 1841 when a report mentioned that the miners were about to use "a large and commodious drying house supplied with warm water."[1] A brief report by John Puckey dated 18th November 1842 indicates the varying depths of the workings: "I have had a long round in the deep part of the mine at Bottrall's shaft, this part of the mine is not looking quite as well, the only good lode is in the end at the 190 west of the shaft on Trathan's lode – the 200 and the other ends are all poor. I like the lode very well in the rise in the back of the 100 fathom level which is now at the 90 fathom level where the lode is large, orey and kindly. The 60 at John's is also improved – the lode is also large and orey. At the old Lanescot we are looking tolerably well, the 80 is rather better, the 100 going west and the 90 going east are both good lodes."

This report also refers to "orey and kindly" lodes at Hodge's shaft, and machinery to work this section was erected in 1843. A 24" whim for Hodge's shaft was purchased from Harveys and delivered to the mine for £520 in March 1843, and an 18" water pressure engine with a column of water 19 fathoms high was also placed in the same shaft, probably at about the same time. The whim engines at Fowey Consols were evidently operated by contract workers, William West telling Harveys in December 1843 that Davis's engine at Bottrall's shaft was kept "full of work" and let to three men at £22 per month. Materials needed to operate the whim were supplied by the mine and these men were charged 8d. for each bushel of coal (94 lbs.), with hemp and gasket 6d. per lb., rape lubricating oil 1/4d. per quart and candles 8d. per lb. The whim and water pressure engine at Bottrall's shaft were felt to be adequate for the immediate development of the eastern section of the mine, supplemented by the installation of a 34' x 5' water wheel for pumping at Pidler's shaft.

At some time towards the end of 1843 the new 80″ engine at Henrietta's shaft was taken down, work in sinking the shaft having been abandoned. The engine had been intended as an investment in the long term future of the mine, but there was a greater need of it at Par Consols where it was re-erected on Treffry's North shaft.[2]

On 25th May 1844 the Mining Journal published a full report on Fowey Consols, part of which was as follows:- "This sett, which is 1,500 fathoms in extent on the run of the lodes, and extending 300 fathoms north and south, is held at 1/24th dues for the western ground, which includes the old Lanescot Mine – and at 1/16th for the eastern part, but which it is expected will be reduced to 1/24th, as the lease is drawing to a close, and negotiations pending for such abatement on renewal. The mine presents at surface the most complete and efficient arrangements for economising labour, the buildings, dressing-floors, &c., with yard for stores and warehouses, smiths' and carpenters' shops, &c., being immediately under the eye and control of the agents.

The principal power employed here is by means of water-wheels and hydraulic-engines. The quantity of water brought to the mine by leats is estimated at not less than 25,000 gallons a minute in the winter season, and about 10,000 in the summer.

The number of lodes discovered and worked upon exceed twenty, of which workings are now being carried on thirteen or fourteen; there are six engine shafts, the principal of which (Austen's) is sunk to a depth of 180 fathoms below adit, which is at this particular point about forty-five fathoms from surface. The quantity of ore sold in 1842 was 12,446 tons, yielding £73,214, or £5.17.6. per ton – the amount divided between the adventurers being £6,400. In the past twelve months ending December, 1843, the total quantity of ore was 13,450 tons, or an excess of about 1,000 tons, which realised £80,856, or £6 per ton – the dividends paid to the adventurers being £9,728; slightly exceeding £200,000 has altogether been realised as surplus, in which, however, is included the reserve fund, applied to working the mine; this is exclusive of the value of the machinery and appliances, which may be fairly estimated at £60,000. The mine, since the great increase of the foreign ores, and the consequent fall in the standard, by stopping numbers of old pitches, which cannot work at a low standard, has fallen off in its surplus returns – the quantity of ores raised in 1838 being 15,771 tons, which yielded £95,190 in money, or £6.0.6. per ton – the dividends declared in which year were £17,408, being nearly double the amount divided in the past year. The number of persons employed is from 1,700 to 1,800, and which may be thus divided:- Agents, engineer, and dialler, 17; tributers, 420; tutworkmen, 310; sumpmen, day labourers, and boys, underground, 175; labourers at surface, paid by day, 180; women, boys and girls, at surface, 670. As illustrative of the economy observed by the application of mechanical power, it may be remarked, that not more than two or three horses are employed.''

Whilst the article attributes the fall in the standard to increasing levels of imported ore an additional reason for the decline was a general slow down in trade in the early 1840s. The main problem faced by the Fowey Consols adventurers however was the exhaustion of many of its richest reserves. The extent to which this was happening is clearly shown in the following production figures:-

	Tons	Proceeds £
Year to 30.6.1844	12,341	66,591
1845	9,809	49,730
1846	8,421	45,586
1847	6,105	32,127

In this short period the ore production declined to levels not seen for more than twenty years, the income halved, and "it became necessary to limit the expenditure of the mine to actually productive work; a pinching economy being required on a mine of such a scale, with such reduced returns, merely to avoid a loss."[3] The fall off in exploratory work underground and output was reflected in the number of people employed which reduced to 920 by the end of 1846.

This was bad enough for the families that depended on Fowey Consols for a living, and worse was to follow. The miners and agricultural labourers of the district were dependant upon potatoes as a substantial part of their diet and for feeding the pigs which they often kept. Potato blight first affected the crop in 1845 and there followed a further crop failure in 1846, with bad corn harvests compounding the problem. The cycle of want and desperation amongst the working population came around again. In January 1847 it was rumoured that the men from Fowey Consols and Par Consols were about to stop a shipment of corn from Par Harbour but Treffry was able to despatch the ship without difficulty. One week later the men at Par Consols were refusing to work and he was asked to attend the setting at Fowey Consols to speak to the miners there. He told them that he regretted the fact that their wages were low in relation to the price of corn and he explained that the mine was not making a profit, its receipts being used to pay for materials and provide the wages for the men. The Mining Journal reported this meeting in its edition of 23rd January 1847 at which Treffry also referred to the proposed final withdrawal of copper import duties and the petitioning of Parliament by interested parties: "Mr. Treffry pointed out to them (the miners) the folly of taking the law in their own hands, either by stopping the shipment of corn or in any other way, adding that if they misconducted themselves they would be still greater sufferers; but that if they behaved orderly and quiet, he could not think Ministers would aggravate their present distress by complying with the petition of the Birmingham manufacturers,[4] and others, which would ruin Fowey Consols and most other deep mines, and throw them all out of work. After Mr. Treffry had thus addressed the Fowey Consols miners they freely took their pitches, and we understand that the Par Consols men also went to work the same morning."

In March seed potatoes and cabbage plants were distributed at Fowey Consols to miners with families and those too poor to buy seed without difficulty.[5] Early in May there was a large increase in the price of corn and this started a series of riots and near riots throughout the county. Treffry was involved in one of the first of these at his small iron mine at Withiel, near Bodmin. Here china clay workers and tin streamers from the St. Austell area tried to persuade his miners to join them as they marched to Wadebridge and Padstow to stop the shipment of grain. He threatened the St. Austell men with arrest, and they left his own men alone.[6] On 14th May handbills were issued from Fowey Consols inviting miners to apply to a relief committee to obtain tickets which would allow them to buy corn at reduced prices, and £200 was also provided by Treffry and the other adventurers to supplement the income of tributers whose gettings had been very low. These efforts to assist the men and their families seem to have been well received, and the immediate area was spared the problems seen elsewhere. At Callington miners intimidated farmers into selling grain to them at their own prices, and in June there were major food riots at Redruth, Pool and St. Austell.[7] These died away in the summer months and a good harvest took some of the edge off the widespread misery. However a letter sent to William Rashleigh in May 1848 from St. Austell still referred to extreme poverty in the neighbourhood and hundreds of destitute families.[8]

At the time of the Withiel disturbance in May 1847 Treffry was 65 years old and there was no sign that the interest he took in his various ventures was waning. In his correspondence he referred to "my constant attendance at my mines, railways etc." Many of his schemes had been conceived when Fowey Consols was at its height and its rapid falling off was a severe blow to his finances. Par Consols did not enter its second very profitable phase until 1848[9] and in April 1847 Treffry mortgaged all his properties, including Place, to raise £80,000.[10] This money was probably used to pay off existing debts. The mansion of Place itself had been a considerable expense to him. In the early 1840s he had built a granite tower and the Porphyry Hall on the western end of the house, the stone used being cut and polished at the porphyry* works at Fowey Consols mine. Some of the stone used came from his quarries at Withiel. Other granites for dressing were brought down from the Luxulyan quarries to Ponts Mill using the Carmears incline leading from the viaduct, and then wound up by water wheel to the mine using the incline built in 1834/35 which terminated near Austen's shaft. Dressed stone fragments found in recent years possibly indicate that the machinery used was driven by the timber-sawing wheel situated near the shaft. The porphyry works remained at the mine until its closure and the sarcophagus of the Duke of Wellington was reputedly processed at the works. This was cut from a 70 ton block of Luxulyanite, a rock with large pink felspar crystals in a black tourmaline groundmass. This block was purchased from the Rashleigh family for £1,100 and is now to be seen in the crypt of St. Paul's Cathedral in London. Whilst men from the mine were probably used to work the stone, a letter in the Royal Cornwall Gazette of 7th May 1858 stated that it was "wrought and polished

*In general terms porphyry refers to rock where relatively large crystals are set in a finer grained groundmass.

Bust of J. T. (Austen) Treffry (1782-1850) at Place House, Fowey.
Sculpted by Neville Northy Burnard.
Reproduced by kind permission of David Treffry.

by steam power" in the field where it was found. With its polished, highly coloured granites the Porphyry Hall at Place is an impressive sight and was seen by Queen Victoria and Prince Albert when they visited the house in September 1846. The granite tower remains a conspicuous landmark in Fowey.

Treffry died on Tuesday 29th January 1850 in his 68th year after catching a severe cold one week earlier. The Mining Journal of 2nd February reported that "although for a considerable period Mr. Treffry had not enjoyed his usual health, not surprising to those who witnessed his mental and bodily exertions, still his death was somewhat sudden, and took his friends by surprise." The West Briton newspaper held Liberal sympathies and only carried a short obituary. Treffry inclined towards the Conservatives as did the Royal Cornwall Gazette and its edition of 1st February was unrestrained in praise of him: "We announce today a general calamity. Mr. Treffry is dead! The enterprise which no difficulty could damp is quenched; the energy which never slept is at rest; the public spirit which expended itself in works of usefulness from which he could never look for a return is passed from among us." It stated that he was the largest employer of labour in Cornwall and mentioned his loyalty to his assistants and his appreciation of their work and that "he saved Fowey Consols from ruin, which threatened it through doubtful prospects, private quarrels, and legal disputes and made it one of the first in the County . . . he valued money only as the means of carrying out his great works, upon which he spent every shilling he received." His funeral was held in Fowey on the morning of the 5th February when nearly all the shops closed at Fowey, Tywardreath and St. Blazey and all work was suspended at his mines, quarries, railways, china clay pits and other works.[11] A correspondent of the Royal Cornwall Gazette[12] reported the funeral: "From an early hour vehicles were seen on the different roads to Fowey. After passing Par the number of pedestrians increased as we went on, but we were not at all prepared for the spectacle that awaited us at Menabilly Lodge, two miles from Fowey. The great body of Mr Treffry's workpeople had formed a kind of regular procession, the men foremost and then the lads and girls, each by themselves with no leaders, but the whole apparently the result of their own arrangements. Among the assembled thousands we saw not one who was not decently and even respectably dressed. The men looked like respectable yeomen, and it was difficult as we observed them to realise that they were common working miners." William Davis was one of the chief mourners, and the bearers connected with Fowey Consols were Thomas Thomas, the mapper and dialler, William Powne, the storekeeper and general clerk, William Polkinghorne, purser's deputy and general pay clerk and John Puckey. It was estimated that there were nearly 10,000 people in Fowey for the funeral, and the miners left the town after the ceremony following an address by John Puckey. Treffry was a bachelor, and left his estate in trust to his cousin, the Rev. Edward J. Wilcocks,[13] providing he took the name of Treffry. The trustee of the estate was James H. Meredith, who had the formidable task of managing a large and complicated business that was burdened by debt.

Although it was being operated on a reduced scale there was plenty of life left in Fowey Consols. It did not declare dividends in the late 1840s, but a cash reserve fund which usually fluctuated between £6,000 and £8,000 enabled it to weather temporary problems and withhold ore from the market when the price was low. The Mining Journal of 24th February 1849 declared "The mine is, upon the whole, looking very well, but it will require at least 12 months from the present time to complete the chief workings now in progress, by extending a deep level from the centre of the mine to the eastern part, where good discoveries have been made, but of which advantage cannot be taken until we have another shaft and steam drawing engine to bring the increased returns of ore to surface." There is no subsequent evidence of a new shaft being sunk or of a new steam whim, and these plans were probably abandoned on cost grounds. By June 1850 a rise in the price of ore had enabled the mine to start paying dividends again,[14] and at the meeting on 18th June the adventurers unanimously passed a resolution "to the effect that the mine having become so deep and hot as to be highly injurious to the constitutions of the miners to have to climb up by ladders, it was considered imperative that they should be drawn up after their days work was finished; and as Pedlar's (Pidler's) shaft could be made available for a man-engine to a depth of 280[15] fathoms from surface, it was determined, for the sake of humanity, to erect such a machine at a cost of £2,160 provided the (mineral) Lords generally will allow out of their future dues 5% per annum on £2,000 (i.e. £100) towards the outlay. This is the more liberal as, during the past 5 years, only £2 per share dividend has been declared; while the outlay has amounted to £204,813.16.1; and the several Lords have been paid £8,125.16.9."[16]

The first man-engine in Cornwall had been installed at Tresavean mine near Lanner in 1842. A man-engine had first been considered for Fowey Consols in the 1830s but no suitable shaft was available. By 1850 it was probably an urgent practical necessity to erect a man-engine in the most suitable shaft at the deep eastern part of the mine to enable the men to go to and from their underground pitches in reasonable physical condition.

It seems that the mineral lords did agree to the small annual reduction in their dues, and the man-engine was subsequently designed and erected by William West and John Puckey.[17] It consisted of an 8" square rod made of Norway pine strapped together end on end which ran from the top to the bottom of the shaft. At every 12 feet there was a 12" square platform attached to the rod with a handle to hold on to, and there were platforms a similar distance apart placed in the shaft on either side of the rod. The rod rose 12 feet on the upstroke of the engine and descended the same distance on the downstroke, with the miners either going down or coming up the shaft by getting on and off the rod on to the platforms in the shaft at each stroke. The rod was raised and lowered with power supplied by a water wheel, 30' x 6' breast, and to ensure a regular motion of the wheel it was geared to a 14 ton flywheel which revolved at three times the rate of the water wheel itself. The circular motion of the wheel was converted into a horizontal motion by means of a crank, this motion was conveyed to the mouth of the shaft by flat rods where it was converted into a vertical motion by being joined to a balance bob, the main rod being joined to the end of the bob. To counterbalance the weight of the rod in the shaft there were three balance bobs in all, the one at the surface and two underground. The water wheel made 5 or 6 revolutions per minute, with the men being able to ascend or descend the 1680' from the surface in about 25 minutes. A celebratory dinner was held in the Fowey Consols Count House on 28th July 1851 to mark the starting of the engine attended by the adventurers, mineral lords and the local gentry together with a Prussian Cabinet minister.[18] Capt. Puckey told the diners that a miner with only one leg had used the engine "with perfect ease." It subsequently became something of a local attraction, with Lord Vivian and his brother using the engine to descend to the bottom

Contemporary drawings of a single rod man-engine similar to the engine at Fowey Consols showing end and side views.

of Pidler's shaft as far as the engine would go, and then down another 20 fathoms by ladders. They then broke some specimens of yellow copper ore before drinking brandy and water on their return to the bottom of the engine. On their safe return to the surface they left "something handsome" with John Puckey for the miners, and according to the Mining Journal of 22nd November, when Puckey asked the miners how they would like to receive their present they unanimously agreed that it should be given to the families whose children had suffered from an outbreak of scarlet fever. The water Lord Vivian used was piped to the bottom of the man engine shaft and some of the levels above for the convenience of the men, and Puckey told the Royal Cornwall Gazette of 19th December 1851: "The miner, instead of being over exhausted and drained dry by perspiration in climbing after his undeground duties, whether by day or night, is now heard expressing himself in ascending to be in paradise . . . we have fixed times for the machine to work and the men to change, and once in the day and night a large body of men meet and pass each other in the shaft on the rod with much regularity; as one steps off on one side in descending, another steps on from the opposite side and ascends with the return stroke."

For the year of 1850 the adventurers had received a dividend of £4 per share on the 494 shares in issue at that time. The reduction from the 512 shares created on the consolidation of Fowey Consols and Lanescot in 1836 occurred in 1848 when a Mr. Field relinquished his holding of 18 shares and received in return a cash payment of £672.2.0.[19] In the first four months of 1851 the mine made a loss of £1,807, principally caused by the expense entailed in the erection of the man engine.[20] One correspondent suggested to the Mining Journal that the managerial costs of the mine were too high and he singled out the purser, who was defended in the Journal in the edition of 2nd August 1851: "Capt. Davis has been long and honourably connected with the adventure, and we think it at least injudicious to recommend his retirement; we do not think his salary disproportionate to the onerous duties which devolve upon him." Throughout 1852 ore production continued to reduce, losses were made and the cash reserve of the mine diminished accordingly. In the early 1850s the British economy was recovering from the recessions of the 1840s and was entering a period of growth accompanied by inflation.[21] The average price per ton of ore received by Fowey Consols in the year ended 30th June 1852 was £5.14.5 and for the year to June 1853 it rose to £7.9.4 yet the losses continued, Davis telling the mine meeting of 14th June 1853: "We have forked the mine of water, which, from the excess of rain last winter, deluged so many of the bottom levels. The prospects are much the same as they were at our last meeting, but the increased prices of materials and labour coupled with the scarcity of tributers in consequence of emigration, and inducements held out to them at home to work in new shallow mines at high wages, prevent our forming any estimate as to future dividends. Although the greatest exertion and economy are being used in trying to make the credits meet expenditure it is evident that this will not be accomplished for the next two or three audits, whatever the result may be afterwards."[22] Whilst the coming of the man engine had eased the working conditions of the miners, the life of the men in the deep levels running east of Bottrall's shaft was extremely hard. It seems clear that all the ore from there had to be trammed back to this shaft to be raised to the surface, and the further the lodes were followed towards Trenadlyn the longer the distance became, ultimately exceeding more than 500 yards. The ventilation in this part of the mine was poor and the underground temperatures very high. It would have been natural for men to leave Fowey Consols for the newer and more prosperous copper mines around Caradon Hill near Liskeard and for the immensely rich Devon Great Consols on the eastern bank of the Tamar near Tavistock. For the more adventurous the New World was also crying out for their skills.

The twin problems of inflation and lack of skilled miners were still making themselves felt in the latter part of 1854 according to a report published in the Royal Cornwall Gazette on 10th November: "Captain Puckey reported that the prospects on the whole were rather better than for some time past. They had some good courses of ore in the deep levels, also a small orey lode in the adit in the north part of the mine, which he thought would lead ultimately to increase the returns and credit; he could not, however, say to what extent beyond the expenditure. The prices of materials were so high, and the majority of miners of inferior class, that although the copper standard was high it was not generally equivalent to the rise in labour, materials etc." Early in 1855 the mine sold an engine for £700, which was probably the 24″ whim engine on Hodge's shaft. In August 1848[23] it was only working for one or two days each week and this part of the mine had evidently come to the end of its productive life. In October 1855 the mine declared a dividend of £2 per share, the payment largely covered by the sale proceeds of the engine, and the mine as a whole was said to be looking "remarkably well." This statement was born out by events, with the ore sales to 30th June 1856 increasing from 4,548 tons in the previous twelve months to a figure of 5,898 tons. This reversed the long downward trend of the output, with the Royal Cornwall Gazette of 18th April 1856 reporting: "The old mine is likely to last many years. Within the last month two new setts have been added on the north part of the property, which are of great importance in future operations . . . a dividend of £1,482 or £3 per share was declared in February out of four months profits and dividends may be considered certain at the next two meetings, while it is probable that discoveries will, in the meantime, be made to enable them to be kept up." It is doubtful if the two setts referred to were new. One was the re-granting of Carruggatt by William Rashleigh Jnr. to J. H. Meredith and William West on behalf of the other Fowey Consols adventurers with dues of 1/18th,[24] and it is probable that the other sett was in the same area of Polharmon/ Carruggatt and granted either by Nicholas Kendall or the Foster family.

In June 1856 the new Mining Exchange at Redruth held its first annual meeting,[25] and it is likely that this prompted the adventurers to sub-divide the shares in October from the existing 494 into 4,940 to create a free market in them as befitted a leading company. In the calendar year of 1856 the mine declared dividends totalling £3,705 and a report by John Puckey in the Mining Journal of 28th February 1857 presents an expectant picture: "The prospects towards the deepest and eastern part of the mine are much the same as for some time past; the best and most valuable shoot of ore has a dip eastward, and is now in the eastern extremity of the 240 crossing the eastern valley, at this point both the lode and dip have shown that much masterly strength has prevailed by the intersection of a very large cross-course, fully 6 feet wide, and that the lode continues to make ore by the dip to the east. This is a very important point for our guidance in regulating the future operations of the mine, but up to this time it is rather premature to decide on the best course to be pursued. From the 210 to the 240 there has been a gradual increase of value in every 10 fathoms in depth; from estimation we find that for 60 fathoms in length to the west of the cross-course from the 210 to the 240, from ores already raised and from what remains to be taken away, we calculate that at £8 per ton (at the present time ore is £10 per ton) the value of the ground is as follows:- from the 210 to the 220, 871 tons of ore value £6,968; from the 220 to the 230, 2,263 tons of ore value 18,104; from the 230 to the 240, 2,693 tons of ore value £21,544. This evidently shows an improvement as we sink the mine. The 250, 260 and 280 fathom levels are being driven with all the force we can apply; the ore from the back of the latter level (supposing it should continue good to that level) cannot all be worked away in less than six years from now. To bring deeper levels into this shoot of ore from the present engine shaft (Bottrall's) will not be prudent or practicable; the estimated expense for every level not being less than £4,000 for manual labour alone. This sum excludes the cost of sinking the shaft, and every such level would require eight years' driving to reach the lode; this being impracticable we must wait longer to see the result of a further development to the east of the cross-course before we determine on the best course to sink it deeper. To the west of Union shaft, at and below the 160, we have some good paying ground, particularly at the present standard which is much in the mine's favour. We have commenced operations in the new sett to the north by driving on two lodes in the adit level which are kindly, producing a little black ore and some malleable copper, apparently indicating that a greater depth is required. Therefore we have also commenced a cross-cut 60 fathoms deep from the adit, to cut the lodes before mentioned and other intermediate lodes, which is a good speculation, and no better course can be adopted.''

A further report by Puckey in the Mining Journal of 27th June 1857 indicates a radical and high cost solution to the problem in the eastern section: "The prospects in the deepest levels eastward in the valley are still favourable. In sinking a winze under the 230, about 5 fathoms before the 240 end, we find the lode considerably improves. The winze is about 5 fathoms deep below the 230, and will produce about 5 tons of ore per fathom, worth about £50. The length of the oreground in the 240, to the east of the cross-course, will by all appearances exceed our expectations, and will produce between the 230 and 240 nearly £25,000. The 280 end is about 50 fathoms behind the 260, therefore we do not expect any ore of importance in that end for two years to come. The lode in the 250 end produces 5 tons of ore per fathom. The fact of every level (supposing them to be 20 fathoms apart) will require eight years to reach the ore from the engine shaft (Bottrall's) is about sufficient to show that some other mode of working need be adopted to develop the eastern part effectually below the 280. To work it in any way should be done with a view to develop it 400 fathoms deep, which will require a spirited outlay in erecting a 70" or 80" engine for pumping, and a 30" whim to work a capstan as well, and a man-machine (man-engine) to lift the miners to the 240 to meet the present man-machine. The subject relative to economy and position for the plant has had a mature consideration, and I would advise the sinking of Henrietta's shaft, and erecting thereon all machinery and pitwork required. To attempt such an undertaking is an effort without precedent in Cornwall, and richly deserves the assistance of everyone interested. To refrain from immediately commencing this work would, in my opinion, be very unwise and injudicious. I advise the new work being set in motion with a full assurance and confidence that if the ore continues down as in the 240 the adventurers will reap a rich reward; and should the ore at any time be found to decline in depth the expenditure on the new operation can be stopped, and the new materials sold to meet a large portion of the outlay. The scheme here proposed can scarcely be called (from the present good appearance of every 10 fathoms in depth producing £25,000 worth of ore) a speculation, but rather an investment of capital to enhance the value of the mine. In the 180 we have found some very good nickel, and have saved for dressing about ½ ton; but it must be further opened on before we shall be able to say what quantity we are likely to raise; it is rich in places, 4" to 10" wide. The western part of the mine, to the west of Union shaft, is kindly to produce ore for several years. The principal workings are chiefly confined to Hewett's lode for 100 fathoms high – that is from the 240 to the 140, and the shaft is being sunk to the 250. We are also driving a long, speculative and expensive cross-cut in the 140, hitherto without success. The north part of the mine in the new sett is being prosecuted vigorously; two lodes are now driving in the adit, but they seem to indicate that the adit is rather too shallow to produce much ore. The 60 cross-cut, towards the same lode, is proceeding satisfactorily. The man-machine continues to work well, and is a very great benefit to the miners working in almost every part of the mine. No other mine of similar extent is better ventilated, and the air is fresh, strong and bracing in all the currents to the utmost extent in the bottom of the mine."[26]

Seen from above, the 280 fathom level passed to the north of, and was within 60 yards of, Henrietta's shaft, and Puckey's report appears to confirm the wisdom of sinking the shaft there in 1836. However, the levels being worked were approximately 170 fathoms below the bottom of Henrietta's shaft and the decision to halt work there in the early 1840s was now affecting the future development of Fowey Consols. If economic deposits of copper were to be found as deep as 400 fathoms this would have been unique in Cornwall, and Puckey hinted at this in his report. It appears that his suggested plans at Henrietta's shaft were supported by the adventurers. At the mine meeting in June 1857 the profit of £1,588 made in the first four months of the year was retained and added to the reserve fund which then totalled £5,702, and this money was to be applied to "the prosecution of works recommended in Capt. Puckey's report."[27] In October the Mining Journal of the 24th reported a postponement of the scheme as follows: "Unforseen circumstances have prevented our immediately proceeding with the work, the fall of the standard being one great cause – for in a mine like this, where there are so many high price pitches at work, it requires, with a fluctuating standard, the greatest possible care and economy to make the returns meet the expenditure. It is our intention, however, to proceed with the work soon, if circumstances will allow. The standard for a few weeks has rallied and somewhat assisted us, but it is presently going back again and therefore great care need again be exercised." The mine made a loss of £1,705 in the last four months of 1857 due to the declining standard,[28] and when John Puckey died at the age of 58 on 27th March 1858 any hope of the proposed ambitious development at Henrietta's shaft probably died with him. Expectations were now centred on Carruggatt.

Notes

1. Report of the Royal Cornwall Polytechnic Society 1841.
2. MJ 25.5.1844. Mining had started at Par Consols in May 1835 by driving exploratory adits north and south through the mile long sett. No machinery for pumping or winding was installed until about 1840, and the first sales of copper ore from the mine did not appear in the ticketing lists until December 1840. By the time of this report in the Mining

Journal the mine had produced approximately 17,300 tons of copper ore which had sold for £131,200, paying dividends of £31,950 to the adventurers. Some of the ore was extremely rich with produce figures of 25 and 28¼ (% of copper metal in the ore), and a 13 cwt. mass of copper ore from the mine was later displayed at The Great Exhibition in London in 1851. In May 1844 the mine had 700 employees and as well as the 80″ engine from Fowey Consols in course of erection it had the following engines under the control of William West:-

Engine	Cylinder	Use
Treffry's	50″	Pumping
Edgcumbe's	24″	Ditto
Carthew's Combined	13″ & 24″	Winding
West's Double	38″ & 22″	Stamping
Stamps & Grinder	30″	Ditto & Grinding
Steam Winder	18″	Winding
Incline	14″	Operating the short incline to Par Harbour & a saw mill.

3. RCG 14.1.1859.
4. In 1850 Britain made 40% of the world's output of manufactured goods that entered international trade. F. Crouzet: The Victorian Economy, 1982.
5. RCG 19.3.1847.
6. RCG 14.5.1847.
7. RCG 11th & 18th June 1847.
8. From T. J. Bennett of Treverbyn which mentioned "the truly lamentable position of the district."
9. MJ Supplement 8.4.1854. To the end of 1845 Par Consols dividends totalled £75,968 with nothing in 1846, £3,072 in 1847 and £44,800 in the following three years. Treffry probably owned 56% of its shares: TF741 at the CRO.
10. TF 1051 and 1052 at the CRO.
11. Treffry was a shareholder in the West of England Clay & Stone Company which went on to become the largest of three companies which amalgamated to form English China Clays in 1919. He died three days before the West of England company made major acquisitions in 1850. R. M. Barton: The Cornish China Clay Industry, 1966.
12. An extensive report of the funeral was carried in the edition of 8.2.1850.
13. Wilcocks did not come from a commercial background. He had been Chaplain of the Scilly Isles, and was Headmaster of Berkhamstead Free Grammar School when Treffry died. RCG 8.2.1850.

14. RCG 29.3.1850. The mine accounts often showed small amounts passing through them relating to Prideaux Wood Mine and West Fowey Consols. In 1857 the Treffry Estate held 4400/6400 of the shares in the former and 4338/6400 in the latter (TF 741 at the CRO). The Cornwall Archaeological Unit report on the Luxulyan Valley has placed Prideaux Wood Mine in the woods north of Ponts Mill, and West Fowey Consols was a larger venture which lay approximately ¼ mile south of Middleway Bridge in St. Blazey. It was at least partly on an old sett known as Wheal Madeline. Both mines were unsuccessful, J. H. Meredith stating in 1856: "At West Fowey Consols £95,000 had been expended without a single shilling to the adventurers." RCG 4.7.1856.

15. In common with other Cornish mines the levels were measured from below the adit which was 40 fathoms deep in this part of the mine. The bottom of the man engine therefore connected with the 240 fathom level.

16. MJ 6.7.1850.

17. MJ 27.12.1851 which also provides the technical details of the man engine.

18. RCG 1.8.1851: "In proposing the toast Mr. Meredith gave a highly interesting account of the first working of the mine, by the late Mr. Treffry, Sir Colman Rashleigh, Bart. and Mr. Pendarves, and of the vicissitudes attendant thereon. He related an anecdote connected therewith showing, that by a mere chance, the late Mr. Treffry became possessed of the greater number of shares in the mine. It appeared that the agent interested in forming the company, after obtaining promises of the cooperation of the individuals above named, found there was still a very large number of shares not taken up. On being asked by the late Mr. Treffry what he intended to do with these shares, he said, 'we mean to put them down to your honour', and so they were put down accordingly." This account bears little or no relation to what actually happened.

19. MJ 24.2.1849.

20. RCG 11.7.1851.

21. One theory for this growth in inflation attributes it to a large increase in the world's gold reserves following its discovery and production in California in 1848 and subsequently in Australia.

22. MJ 25.6.1853.

23. I am grateful to Ken Brown for access to his copy of Browne's Engine Reporter for August 1848. The Fowey Consols engines had been removed from Lean's Engine Reporter at the end of 1845 following a dispute about the weight of the kibbles used at Par Consols and Fowey Consols. Browne's did not enjoy the same good reputation as Lean's for unbiased reporting. D. B. Barton: The Cornish Beam Engine, 1965.

24. R 4912 at the CRO. Another sett (Menabilly Wheal Rashleigh) was granted by Rashleigh to Meredith and West relating to land on the eastern side of Par Beach. (R4913).
25. RCG 20.6.56.
26. The last sentence in this report would appear to have been prompted by a report to the Royal Cornwall Polytechnic Society by Dr. Richard Quiller Couch in 1857. His report highlighted the short life expectancy of miners in St. Just, partially caused by chest complaints brought on by poor air underground. Puckey's comments were contradicted by much of the evidence given to the Parliamentary Commission of 1864 – see Chapter VII.
27. RCG 26.6.1857.
28. RCG 2.4.1858.

THE FINAL YEARS

AFTER PUCKEY'S death the mine reports appearing in the Mining Journal were signed by Captains Philip Rich, C. Merrett and Samuel Sampson. Many of the tribute pitches in the old parts of the mine were deep and difficult to work and the tributers there were receiving 14/- or 15/- in the pound (£) for every pound's worth of ore raised,[1] so this left very little for the adventurers. The importance of finding new copper deposits was highlighted in a Fowey Consols report which appeared in the Royal Cornwall Gazette of 25th February 1859: "We regret to say that many of our old pitches are fast wearing out; and, were it not for the recent improvements in the mine, our returns would materially diminish. Should our present bright prospects continue, and discoveries be made in the lands recently added to our sett, and of which there are strong grounds to hope for, it will be necessary to incur a considerable expense in new machinery before the adventurers can derive any pecuniary benefits from them. Therefore it would be encouraging false hopes to calculate on an early resumption of dividends; but we hope and believe that at no very distant period we may calculate on a good dividend paying mine." Over the years in the western part of the sett at Wheal Hope several shallow shafts and trials had been largely unsuccessful, the adits driven into the mine from the south had tried that ground and there were no new discoveries to the east. In the north western part of the sett an exploratory level had been driven north for more than 400 yards from Anthony's shaft towards Penpillick[2] without making any finds, and now hopes again rested on the north eastern part of the sett at Carruggatt. Development work seems to have restarted there early in 1857, the adventurers convincing themselves that they could succeed where J. T. Treffry had previously failed. A reference in the Mining Journal of 30th October 1858 to "the lode in the adit level driving west in Foster's (Carruggatt?) wood" is probably an indication that Richard Foster's wish in the 1830s to have an adit driven into the sett from the eastern valley was now being met.

The improvements anticipated in the Gazette of 25th February 1859 soon came about. The last dividend paid by the mine had been 6/- per share (£1,482 in total) declared in February 1857 based on profits made at the end of 1856. In the last four months of 1859 Fowey Consols made a profit of £870 and followed this with another profit of £754 in the ensuing four months, dividends of 2/6d per share (£617.10.0) being paid on each of these amounts. The 20″ whim engine on Trathan's shaft was moved to Kendall's North shaft at Polharmon, the mine report stating[3] that it was "to develop the lodes in Carruggatt and Polharmon estates, in the former of which they had a very promising lode in the adit level for more than 50 fathoms. In the 60 they had cut a lode, but could not drive on it for want of ventilation. They strongly recommended its being driven on which, however, could not be done before the shaft was holed." William Davis was now nearly 70 years old, and with the mine apparently entering a more prosperous period he let it be known that he wished to retire as purser, retaining an income of £300 per annum from the mine as the auditor of its books. The substantial sum involved raised some eyebrows, a letter from William Polking-horne (the deputy purser) in June 1860 stating: "The major, I understand from Mr. Treffry, has made up his mind to continue the pursership for the present in consequence of Mr. Treffry telling him his views." This seems to refer to Charles E. Treffry, the son of the Rev. E. J. Treffry, who had been pencilled in as a possible replacement for Davis. Charles was only 18 years old, and it could well be his reluctance to take on the post that persuaded Davis to stay on. The Mining Journal of 30th June 1860 carried the following underground report: "Trathan's lode: in the 280, east of Bottrall's shaft, the lode is large and poor. In the 270 the lode is 2½ feet wide, but poor. The lode in the 260 is 3 feet wide, and will yield 1½ tons of ore per fathom. In the 250 and 240 the lode is poor. Bottrall's lode: in the 260 the lode is 2½ feet wide, and will yield 1½ tons of ore per fathom. In the 240 and 230 the lode is poor. Anne's lode: in the 170 the lode is 3 feet wide, and will yield 2 tons of ore per fathom. Hewett's lode: in the 200, west of Union shaft, the lode is 1½ feet wide, and will yield 1 ton of ore per fathom. In the 180 the lode is 2 feet wide, and will yield 1½ tons of ore per fathom. In the 170 east the lode is 1½ feet wide, and will yield 1 ton or ore per fathom. In the 160, east and west of Ray's shaft, the lode is poor. John's lode: In the 100, 90, and 80, east of Cocks[4] (Coates's?) shaft, the lode is large, and containing a little ore. Coleman's lode: in the 40, east of West's shaft, the lode is 1½ feet wide and will yield 1 ton of ore per fathom. In the 24 the lode is small and poor. The lode in the rise west of Carruggatt shaft is 3 feet wide, and containing a little ore, but not sufficient to value. The other bargains and pitches not mentioned are much as usual." No further dividends had been paid in 1860, and the reserve fund was reduced to £3,324 at the end of the year[5] following a loss of £1,407 in the period September/December. The average price received for each ton of ore dropped 13/6d to £6.9.0 during the last six months of the year. Fowey Consols was still employing 740 people[6] (530 men, 80 boys and 130 girls) and the amount of copper ore sold in the year ending June 1861 at 4,914 tons was still holding up well, with a profit of £447.4.0. made in the period September to December 1861. The mine was now under the management of John Puckey's nephew, Francis. He was 50 years old and had originally worked at Fowey Consols between 1826 and 1836, and since 1842 he had been a captain at Par Consols.[7]

For the miners 1862 started with an enquiry into their religious habits, the Royal Cornwall Gazette of 3rd January 1862 reporting: "at the monthly setting of Fowey Consols mines, on Saturday last, a complaint was made of the manner in which a great portion of the miners regarded the Sabbath. Mr. (Rev. E.J.?) Treffry gave them a good lecture, and informed them that at the next setting day he should expect every man to declare himself to what denomination he belongs, which will be inserted in a book, and their attendance at their different places of worship enforced, if they intend working there; and that the same rule will be carried out in the other mines where he is interested. He hoped there were no infidels present; if so, they had better part at once." The year marked a period of declining copper sales and ore prices and was notable for another visit from a Parliamentary Commission. This Commission was appointed to enquire into the health and safety of miners and it eventually published its report in 1864.[8] Its investigations were carried out at a time of rising concern about the working conditions underground in Cornwall and the evident poor health of many of the miners who worked there. Of the then current workforce at Fowey Consols Francis Puckey and the surgeon W.

W. Tayler were interviewed, together with William Petherick and John Sampson, a miner who had left the mine in 1846. The detailed report of the Commissioners provides an insight into the working conditions underground in the mines' final years.

Commenting on the general health of Cornish miners the Commissioners reported: "In examining, even casually, a large number of miners, it is impossible not to be struck with the peculiarly delicate appearance of many of them, and especially the older men and of the boys and young men who have worked underground for only a short time. Instead of having the bright and clear complexions of the young people employed at surface, those who labour in the mines have a very pale sallow appearance, and this they seem to acquire even after having worked underground only for a few months. The middle-aged men (i.e. in their 20s) are less unhealthy looking but those who have long worked in the mines and are verging towards old age have a prematurely old appearance, a stooping gait, and an anxious expression of countenance. They are thin, pale, and sallow, and have peculiarly dingy complexions. For men following a laborious occupation they are by no means muscular, and very generally their pulse at the wrist is feeble . . . Comparatively few men are found at work who have passed the middle period of life, and still fewer who under such circumstances appear and report themselves to be in good health." The main reason for the generally poor health and short working life was the very hard physical labour in badly ventilated and hot working places. Fowey Consols was no different in this respect from other Cornish mines. By this time the scale of the underground workings was enormous, with an estimated 7 miles of shafts and 150 miles of levels beneath the surface.[9] The average age of the 346 men working underground at the time of the Report was 29 years and 3 months, and this compares with an average age of 28 years 11 months for 17,037 miners working in a total of 191 mines in Cornwall and Devon. Puckey told the Commission that the mine was then 300 fathoms deep under the adit and that the deepest level being worked was the 270 fathom level. A pare of six men were employed there and they were supplied by air from a shaft (probably Bottrall's) 400 yards away. The air temperature in this level was 94° Fahrenheit. Puckey said that the mine resorted to artificial means of ventilation when candles refused to burn or when powder smoke lay in a level after blasting or when it became too hot. There was no definition given of what was considered too hot. Underground doors were used to control ventilation which could be affected by the direction of the wind at surface. Petherick stated "In summer time, when the temperature ranges from 75° to 95° (Fahrenheit) then the atmosphere is so heavy below that the heat rushes down, and destroys the ventilation, as it cannot escape through the shaft." John Sampson recalled working at Fowey Consols 16 years previously in a place where the air was dead, and the ventilation was by a stream of water flowing through a series of pipes which forced air into his pitch. When asked by the Commission if the men caught cold he replied "Yes, I believe that the men caught cold by sitting in the footways more than anything else. That is the tutwork men, the tributers would also catch cold, because they had miserable places to change at Fowey Consols when I was there, they had miserable little barracks. I do not know if this has altered since I came away."

The Commission described the various changing houses on the mine as "dirty in the extreme." If the tutworkers came up before time they would be spaled 2/6d., and Sampson said that they sometimes waited up to ¾ hour in the footways waiting for the bell to ring if they could not get back to their pitch after blasting. The taking of watches underground was positively discouraged, and the only other way to judge the passing of time was by the burning of candles. The coming of the man engine in 1851 had lessened the strain on the men working in the deep eastern part of the sett, and Petherick spoke of his experiences in climbing ladders prior to its installation. He said "I recollect going up from the 140 fathom level, and when I got within 50 fathoms of the surface I would as soon lie down and remain as go up, I was so exhausted; that principally arose from the inclined state of the ladders; they were inclined in that way that the weight rested upon the chest and head." In 1862 the man engine was worked for 1½ to 2 hours at 6 a.m., 2 p.m. and 10 p.m., and also at 8 a.m. for the tributers to descend and at 5 p.m. to bring them up. Puckey felt that the men preferred to wait 3 or 4 hours to use the engine rather than climb approximately 1,800 feet of ladders. He said that he had found a great improvement in the miners' health following its introduction.

Puckey did concede that, on average, men only worked to the age of 40 or 45 which was the normal age for death, but many men were older than that, and some worked until 60 years of age.

William Tayler[10] told the Commission that men did not continue to work long after their 40th birthday: "it is soon after that the health of many begins to fail." He also said "I recollect that there used to be from 15 to 20 persons receiving permanent pay from the mine on account of heart disease and consumption, and now I do not think there are above 5 or 6, if so many, in consequence of the substitution of the man-engine." The Commission was, however, to be supplied with figures from the Registrar General's office showing that at age 35, a Cornish miner was about three times more likely to die within the next 10 years of life from consumption or lung disease than a man employed in the better ventilated coal mines of Durham, Northumberland or Staffordshire, and by age 45 the likelihood was a factor of over four.[11]

The Commission eventually published its report in July 1864 and it made recommendations to improve the working lives of Cornish miners, including better ventilation underground. Faced with the possibility of legislation that would considerably increase their costs many of the mining interests in Cornwall opposed the measures. A petition was sent to the House of Lords objecting to the recommendations by "Adventurers in British Copper, Lead and Tin Mines, and Merchants and Manufacturers and others interested in Mines in the Districts of Par, St. Blazey, Tywardreath and their Vicinities". Confronted with considerable opposition to the proposed Bill and the proximity of a general election the Liberal government felt unable to support it in Parliament, and the Metalliferous Mines Bill never passed into law.[12]

In 1862 the adventurers seem to have finally given up hope at Carruggatt. In November the mine paid a dividend, 2/10d. per share, which was said to be the proceeds of the sale of part of Carruggatt and Polharmon setts and materials sold to Nicholas Kendall and others at a price of £700.[13] This sale would appear to have included the whim engine on Kendall's North shaft. There was obviously a difference of opinion between Kendall and the Fowey Consols adventurers about the potential at Carruggatt, and the latter's predicament was summarised in the report appearing in the Mining Journal of 7th March 1863. The accounts for the last four months of 1862 had shown a loss of £1,435.17.7 which reduced the reserve fund to £1,340 and the Journal stated: "The chief cause of this unfavourable state of affairs is the falling off in the eastern part of the mine, on Bottrall's and Trathan's lodes. The drop in the standard makes a difference of £1 per ton of ore as compared with twelve months since.'' The mine had weathered many economic recessions in the past but the decline in the eastern section effectively sealed its fate. The income from copper sales at £20,863.19.0. for the year ended June 1863 was down approximately 1/3rd on the receipts of two years previously, and as well as cutting their losses at Carruggatt the adventurers were also economising on the exploratory tutwork underground. In October the parts of the sett owned by Kendall and John Tremayne came up for renewal and these were only granted on the understanding that more tutwork would be carried out. Further losses had reduced the reserve fund to £971, and to carry out this additional work it was recognised that the adventurers would probably have to contribute to the costs from their own pockets by paying a call. The Mining Journal of 31st October 1863 quoted from the mine report: "The underground operations stipulated by Messrs. Kendall and Tremayne to be done in consideration of new leases being granted by them are such as hold out a reasonable prospect of being ultimately highly remunerative, though, of course, an additional monthly outlay must be incurred for some time to come in developing the objects contemplated. In accordance therewith we, on Saturday last, put on the extra tutwork in various parts of the mine. On the whole our prospects are rather better than at the last general meeting of the adventurers.''

These adventurers were now seeing the familiar pattern which heralded the closure of many Cornish mines – the necessity of calls and a request to the mineral lords for an abatement in dues. At the mine meeting of October 1864 there was another loss of £524.15.4 to report on the four months ending August, and "from the present poverty of the mine, coupled with the fact that for the last four years, notwithstanding the credits for ores etc. totalling £117,246.2.6 (upon which dues amounting to £4,571.0.6 have been paid to the lords of the soil), it has been worked at a loss to the adventurers of £3,936.4.9: therefore, before sanctioning the outlay as contemplated in the agents' report (about 10/- per share), the purser was instructed to make an application to the several lords and ladies of the soil for such a reduction of the dues as from the present and probable future condition of the mine may appear to be equitable.''[14] The income referred to would have covered the calendar years and included not only receipts from copper but also money received for small amounts of iron pyrites, tin, silver, zinc and nickel produced from time to time. Thomas Spargo, a Cornish mining engineer and share broker, commented on the agents report of October: "at the time of writing it almost all the workings were so poor as to show the value of the lodes to have been only from £3 to £6 per fathom, except in one instance where a side lode was producing £12 per fathom; yet by backing the agent's judgment in attacking the side lodes, and working upon the liberality of the lords, who ought without scruple or delay to abate the dues, with the very moderate calls the agents propose, we agree with the agents that this may be considered a good and safe speculation."

The workforce was now down to 350:- 250 men, 50 women and girls and 50 boys.[15] In February 1865 the first call was made[16] since J. T. Treffry took control of the mines more than 45 years previously. This was at the rate of 7/6d. per share with another call of 3/6d. per share made in the following June. In the year ended 30th June 1865 Fowey Consols sold only 3,247 tons of copper ore at a low average of £4.16.5 per ton which realised £15,659. The reduced price was an indication of poorer quality ore rather than a low standard. With some of the mineral lords apparently reluctant to reduce their dues temporarily it was decided that the majority shareholder, the Treffry Estate, should approach them in company with the purser to ask them to suspend entirely all the dues for the time being, rather than just reduce them temporarily. William Polkinghorne, the deputy purser, wrote on 25th August 1865: "Thousands of pounds will be received by the Estate if the mine be suspended and the materials sold when times become more brisk; whilst the whole will be frittered away, with the addition of thousands of pounds to the Estate in calls, unless one or two good and permanent discoveries can soon be made; but of which, I am sorry to say, there is no certainty." The Estate still held 3,930 of the 4,940 shares in issue and those shareholders not willing to pay calls had to relinquish their shares. According to Polkinghorne "There will be hundreds of relinquishments before another meeting, and nearly the whole mine will belong to the Estate." The two Trustees of the Treffry Estate were now R. T. Head of Exeter and Edward Lambert of London who had been appointed after the death of J. H. Meredith in 1857. William Davis had finally handed in his notice, and on 20th June 1865 Head wrote to Lambert: "The only proper person to fill the office (of purser) is Mr. Polkinghorne.

Major Davis said he did not wish to retire until the six months mentioned in his notice, and of course no one could call on an officer who had served the mine for 40 years to retire before he chose to do so. Another thing I felt was just – viz. that a purser who had served so long and during whose service the adventurers had earned £200,000 was entitled to some retiring pension but as the mine is too poor now to admit of this, the pension can only come out of the salary of the newly appointed purser." One of Davis's last official duties was to welcome Royal visitors to Fowey.

On the morning of July 22nd 1865 The Prince and Princess of Wales (Albert Edward, the future Edward VII, and Alexandra) arrived in Fowey on board the Royal yacht Osborne. They came ashore at Albert Quay, following in the footsteps of Queen Victoria and Prince Albert when they visited the town in 1846. William Davis formally welcomed the Royal party with a speech, and after being shown the Porphyry Hall at Place the party went next to Par to see the smelting works there. They then travelled up to Fowey Consols where they were again met by Davis and conducted around by William West and the mineral agent of the Duchy of Cornwall, Capt. John Simmons. He was no stranger to the mine having worked there from 1844 until he took up his post with the Duchy in 1857.[17] The party was shown Austen's 80″ engine which was described in the newspaper report of the visit, probably at West's suggestion, as the most powerful single pumping engine in the world. A presentation was made of some mineral specimens and the man engine was shown in operation, the Princess being instrumental in ensuring that a gift was given to the men who worked it. The West Briton of 28th July reported: "The Prince and Princess were loudly cheered, and by none more than the Cornish girls, tanned by the sun and overflowing with health and spirits, who work on the surface of the mines, and in whose demonstrations of delight the Princess seemed to take much pleasure."

Despite the tidying up which no doubt preceded the arrival of the Royal party it must have been obvious that the mine was only a shadow of its former self, and the visit proved to be a bright spot in an increasingly gloomy picture. In September 2/3rds. of the mineral lords agreed to give up their dues for twelve months,[18] but in October the adventurers had to pay another call of 3/6d. per share, making total calls of 14/6d. per share in 1865. Another payment of 3/6d. was requested at the February 1866 meeting, and it was at this gathering that Major William Davis R.M. (as he preferred to be known) finally retired as the purser. He was 75 years old and it is not known if he ever received a pension from the mine. He was replaced by William Polkinghorne, William West's son-in-law. Davis lived on until 1873.

Fowey Consols was now on its last legs and nationally 1866 was a year of growing economic difficulty, the collapse of the London bank of Overend, Gurney in May causing financial panic and very high interest rates which contributed towards an eventual slump. At the mine another call of 3/- per share was made at the June meeting, the Mining Journal of 30th reporting: "The lords of the soil are earnestly requested to continue a remission of dues as it will be to their advantage to assist in keeping the mine going during the present depression. Captains (Francis) Puckey, Merrett and Job say 'from the continued depressed state of the Metal Market, and the consequent low standard for copper ores in addition to our not having yet succeeded in making any good discoveries our returns have fallen off. In order to lessen the costs we have suspended about one month since a portion of our unproductive operations, thereby lessening the costs underground and at surface by about £150 per month.' The captains fully hope that the adventurers will yet again be repaid for their outlay." This proved to be a forlorn hope, the evident reduction in costs being insufficient to avoid an additional call of 3/6d. in October. The whole huge sett had been intensively mined for more than 40 years and there was probably nothing left to find: "The ground has been thoroughly mined in both and all directions, from the centre to the circumference, most of the veins wholly giving up both east and west in a mineral bearing sense, and terminating in mere strings, leaders and interlaminations and ceasing to be lodes in the true sense. Westwards more especially the remnants of the group of lodes were pursued to points beyond barrenness."[19]

The Royal Cornwall Gazette of 28th February 1867 reported the mine meeting which effectively described the end of Fowey Consols: "A general meeting of the adventurers was held on the mine on the 19th inst., the Rev. Dr. Treffry in the chair. The accounts for four months ending December were passed, and a balance of £813.11.11 was carried to the debit of the next account. A call of 3/- per share was made. The purser reported that a prospectus had been prepared for working the south ground under the designation of the South Fowey Consols Copper Mine. The agents reported as follows: "Since the last general meeting of the adventurers we have, as per resolutions then passed, suspended all our tutwork and tribute operations in the deep parts of the mine; we have been for some time past, and still are, drawing up the materials from there. At Bottrall's we have taken up all the railroads, pitwork, pumps, rods, underground bobs, ladders etc. from the 300 fathom level as high as the 70 fathom level and expect to take up the remaining portion of the rods etc. in the shaft by the end of the present week. At Union shaft we have taken up the railroads, pumps, rods, bearers and cisterns, also the casing and dividing of the shaft, ladders etc. from the 250 fathom level as high as the 100 fathom level, and have now commenced taking up the man engine rods, the casing and dividing, ladders etc. from the bottom of the man engine shaft, viz. the 240 fathoms level, and as soon as we have taken up the same to the 140 fathoms level, which will take fully a week from this time, we shall then commence operations in taking up the pitwork etc. from the bottom of Austen's shaft and then stop the engine for some time. The expense of what has been done has considerably increased the charges for sundry work during the past four months. In the remaining shallow levels above the 60, we have now only 36 tributers at work, and according to our present prospects we shall rise from 50 to 60 tons of copper ore per month (worth say £4.10.0. per ton) besides a little stamps' ore and slimes." The decision to bring matters to a conclusion was probably not a difficult one. The adventurers had been asked to pay calls totalling £1.7.6 per share over a two year period and with the copper ore from the mine fetching less than £4 per ton there was no end in sight to the repeated calls.

The mine materials and equipment were auctioned on Monday July 15th 1867 and appear to have been purchased entirely by William West.[20] Much of the machinery from the great days thirty years previously had remained on the sett, including Austen's 80″ pumping engine and the steam whims at Bottrall's (Davis's engine), Powne's and Ray's shafts. 22″ water pressure engines were installed in Union and Bottrall's shafts until the end, and together with the 80″ pumping engine they had been the prime means of keeping the vast underground workings unwatered in the final years of the mine. West was still the engineer at Fowey Consols, but he was now a prosperous entrepreneur whose main interests lay elsewhere.[21] The ultimate fate of his famous 80″ engine is unknown. Many water wheels remained on the mine after closure and seven of them were again advertised for sale in the Mining Journal of 19th March 1870. Ore would have been recovered from the burrows after the mine closed,[22] and it is possible that they were retained for this purpose and to process the ore produced at the unsuccessful South Fowey Consols mine.[23] The following details from the Redruth ticketing of 29th August 1867 show the last ores sold under the name of Fowey Consols:-

Tons	Purchasers	Price per ton
43	Vivian & Sims	£1.11.6
39	Vivian, Grenfell & Sims	£5.15.6
36	ditto	£3.12.6
2	Sims, Willyams & Co	£28. 1.0

And so Fowey Consols came to an end. Par Consols was being operated at a very reduced level until it was wound up in 1870, just one more statistic marking the rapid decline of the Cornish copper mining industry. Whilst the newer mines in the east of the county were able to struggle on against falling copper prices caused by the growing level of imports, the old, deep mines were nearly exhausted and unable to survive. In some mines, notably around Camborne, tin was found beneath the copper, giving these mines a bright future after weathering the economic slump of the late 1860s. Mining was ended as a significant source of employment in Tywardreath and St. Blazey, and these parishes shared in the general destitution prevalent amongst most of the mining population of Cornwall in the years of 1867 and 1868.[24] A Cornwall County Distress Fund Committee was set up, and the Royal Cornwall Gazette of 30th January 1868 reported on a fund-raising evening of entertainment at Bodmin Guildhall "on behalf of the distressed miners and their families at Tywardreath." The hall was said to have been filled to overflowing, and the Rev. J. D. Hawksley of Tywardreath told the audience that "he never expected to see such distress as there was at Tywardreath. If he were to say that many of them were starving it would not be more than one iota more than was really the case." On 20th February the same newspaper referred to the fact that there were 345 people earning on average 1/1d. per week per person

Photos of Henrietta's Engine House taken November 1969 and November 1996. The extension of 1996 represents the site of the original boiler house.

in the parish, a figure that was half the sum that it would have cost to maintain them in a workhouse. The Distress Fund Committee encouraged emigration and 8,000 miners had recently left Cornwall, leaving 20,000 dependants behind them. The long term effects were such that between the Census of 1871 and that of 1881 the population of Cornwall decreased by 9% to 330,686.

The recorded production of ore from Fowey Consols shows sales of 28 tons of tin ore, 46 tons of zinc ore, 8 tons of nickel ore and 2287 tons of iron pyrites.[25] In round figures it sold 383,000 tons of copper ore which raised £2.25 million. With its abundant mineral wealth the dividends to the adventurers of £212,730 could be considered moderate by the standards of some other Cornish copper mines. John Taylor held the lease of the Consolidated Mines at Gwennap from 1819 until 1840 and during this time the value of the ore it sold was also £2.25 million but the dividends to the adventurers amounted to £480,156. Tresavean mine at Lanner near Redruth was said to have paid dividends totalling £450,000 before 1846 and even these sums were far eclipsed by Devon Great Consols near Tavistock which paid its adventurers £1,225,216 between 1845 and 1903. However in each case these other mines were mainly sustained by one great lode of copper.[26] Fowey Consols was working on 16 distinct lodes at its peak in 1838, and their discovery and development increased its costs accordingly. Today the mine is principally remembered for its extensive use of water power, the engine trial of 1835 and for the remarkable entrepreneur whose creation it was. Through him the money generated by the mine was largely spent in his adopted county, and it left the legacy of Par Harbour to the china clay industry of the 20th century and a railway line to serve it.[27]

There is little evidence now remaining at surface to give a true impression of the past scale of this great undertaking. It is fortunate that the two 80″ pumping engine houses still stand on Fowey Consols today, Henrietta's to mark the labours of the miners who worked in the formidable conditions in the deep eastern part of the mine, and Austen's, which survives (albeit in a state of increasing decay) as a memorial on the mine to the man whose name it bears, and whose personality and enterprise so dominated its history.

Photograph of Austen's Engine House in 1995 (top) and part of the Northern incline in 1969 where it crossed the road to Ponts Mill (below).

Note

At the time of writing the engine house at Henrietta's shaft is being sympathetically converted into a private residence and its future appears secure. The Trevithick Society has a long standing ambition to conserve Austen's engine house but the cost is currently estimated at around £30,000. Most of the waste burrows on the mine have been either removed or much reduced in size to provide road building material and much of the site has been grassed over. The bottom end of both inclines from the mine to the original canal basin can be viewed from near the top of Penpillick Hill. One side of the buttress still exists where the northern incline crossed the road to Ponts Mill and the remains of a burrow on the northern side of the road marks the site of the waste from the Wheal Hope stamps. The Fowey Consols sett is situated on private property and it is fortunate that the significant remains can be viewed from the neighbouring roads and public footpaths. Please take care at all times. The Luxulyan Valley still contains the leat system, viaduct and Carmears incline built by Treffry more than 150 years ago. Access is available, and a full survey of this area was published by the Cornwall Archaeological Unit in 1988 under the title "The Luxulyan Valley". The Par Canal is traceable for much of its length, and although the lead smelter is long gone the port of Par is still used today for the export of china clay.

Notes

1. Evidence given by J. H. Meredith to the Committee on the Rating of Mines. RCG 4.7.1856.
2. From the underground plans of Fowey Consols held at the CRO, ref MRO R98-N21.
3. RCG 27.2.1857, MJ 3.3.1860, RCG 6.7.1860. The 1881 Ordnance Survey Map 1/2500 shows a disused engine house on Kendall's North shaft.
4. There appears to be no 'Cock's' shaft shown on the mine plans.
5. MJ 29.6.1861.
6. Thomas Spargo: Statistics and Observations on the Mines of Cornwall and Devon, 1864.
7. Evidence given on 22.4.1862 to the Parliamentary Commission on Health and Safety in non coal mines, report published 1864.
8. The Chairman of the Commission was a Scottish landowner, Lord Kinnaird, and of the six other Commission members four were Cornish Members of Parliament including Nicholas Kendall, the Conservative

M.P. for East Cornwall. The Commission and its findings are analysed in "Cornish Mine Labour and the Royal Commission of 1864" by C. Schmitz, Journal of the Trevithick Society No. 10 (1983).

9. MJ 14.4.1860. According to Francis Puckey there were 40 miles of underground tramways at one time at Fowey Consols. The RCG of 19.3.1847 gives a figure of 50 miles.

10. In 1862 William W. Tayler attended the miners in Tywardreath and William Pace dealt with those in St. Blazey.

11. Per C. Schmitz as above.

12. ibid.

13. X 55/17 held at the CRO.

14. MJ 29.10.1864.

15. As for Note 6 but 1865 edition.

16. X 55/17 held at the CRO.

17. RCG 19.6.1857.

18. MJ 23.9.1865.

19. Letter to the MJ 19.2.1881 signed "A Miner".

20. See Appendix III. Copies of a few sheets from the mine reports in the period 1868/69 still exist and were shown to the writer by Derek Reynolds of the Par Old Cornwall Society. They detail the efforts made to tidy up the sett and some of the dividends paid to the adventurers following the sale. Although incomplete they contain the following entry: "Received of Wm. West the 3rd instalment of the purchase of all the machinery and other effects of the mine sold by public auction on 15th July 1867, balance £1,216.13.4." Dividends known to have been paid from the proceeds are 4/- per share in 1868 and 2/- per share in 1869.

21. West had his own foundry at St. Blazey and was a partner in The Liskeard & District Bank at Liskeard and The South Cornwall Bank at St. Austell.

22. £706 was received for copper ore recovered from the burrows in 1882. R. Symons: The Gazetteer of the County of Cornwall, 1884.

23. The mine closed in the early 1870s. The adventurers gave six months notice in June 1873 that they were giving up the use of the Fowey Consols leat. TF 959 at the CRO.

24. The following figures from "British Mining" by Robert Hunt, published in 1884, illustrate the decline in the output and copper standard for the Cornish mines:-

Year	Production tons	Average standard
1860	180,448	£133. 8.0
1865	159,409	£122.12.0
1870	81,278	£98. 1.0

The economic and social background are covered in "Cornwall in the Age of the Industrial Revolution" by Dr. John Rowe, first published in 1953 and "A History of Copper Mining in Cornwall & Devon" by D. B. Barton, published 1961.

25. Memoirs of the Geological Survey – Bodmin & St. Austell, HMSO 1909.

26. The figures for the Consolidated Mines at Gwennap were obtained from "History of Gwennap" by C. C. James. D. B. Barton's "The Redruth & Chasewater Railway 1924–1915" gives figures of 299,184 tons of copper ore sold for £2,099,485 with dividends of £480,000. Taylor was not permitted to renew his lease at Gwennap Consols and spent the last two years of the lease using all his resources to strip the mine of its available ore reserves, having abandoned exploratory work. Tresavean's wealth was founded on a great shoot of ore which went down from the 120 fathom level to the 310. The main lode at Devon Great Consols was enormously rich and the mine produced a total of 742,000 tons of copper ore.

Par Consols was instanced in the 'Gazetteer' mentioned in Note 22 as the Cornish mine giving the quickest return to its adventurers. The Treffry Estate owned 3600/6400 (56%) of the shares in 1857 and it is interesting to compare its performance with that of Fowey Consols, both mines being under the same management. The following figures were obtained from "The Memoirs of the Geological Survey" which lists Lanescot Mine separately:-

	Copper ore tons	Average produce	Tin ore tons
Fowey Consols	319,790	7.8%	28
Lanescot	63,123	8.1%	
Par Consols	122,689	9.1%	3,785

Par Consols is generally said to have paid dividends of £250,000 to its adventurers (MJ 15.7.1882). The Mining Journal of 8.4.1854 states that dividends of £149,120 had been paid to the end of December 1853, apparently from only 80,000 tons of copper ore produced to that date.

Its produce figure indicates that, on average, its copper ore was 12% richer than Lanescot's and 17% richer than the ore mined at Fowey Consols. It was also a much shallower mine than Fowey Consols, being 210 fathoms deep in its deepest eastern section (J.H. Trounson: Cornwall's Future Mines, 1993) which had clear cost implications. Significant amounts of tin ore were found beneath the copper in the western part of the mine, the production of this ore being primarily in the period from 1855 until the mine was finally wound up in 1870.

27. To avoid the Luxulyan Viaduct and Carmears incline the railway was re-routed in the 1870s through the valley by the Cornwall Minerals Railway.

THE CORNWALL HERITAGE TRUST
AND THE TREFFRY VIADUCT

Robert Symons, a Land and Mineral Surveyor, was a frequent contributor to the Mining Journal in the 1880s. The edition of 15th July 1882 quoted a lengthy letter from him on the subject of J. T. Treffry as "the executor, unaided, of works of costly magnitude, and of great utility." He concluded by stating "Mr. Treffry was a successful speculator, and a man of singular energy, but if Fowey Consols instead of being a productive mine had turned out otherwise the great works which he accomplished would not have been known, but having been accomplished his memory will remain coeval (contemporary) with the granite blocks which constitute the viaduct in Luxulyan Valley."

The viaduct is now in the care of the Cornwall Heritage Trust, a Charity (Regd. No 291607) which has the costly responsibility of managing and maintaining many sites of importance in Cornwall. If you wish to play a part in preserving the viaduct as a monument to an exceptional man and his times please send your donation or request for membership of the Trust to:-

Jim Lewis (CHT)
c/o Lloyds Bank Plc
Central Square
Newquay
Cornwall TR7 1JB

APPENDIX I

SALES OF COPPER ORE

	WHEAL TREASURE			LANESCOT		
Year Ended	Tons of Ore (21 cwts.)	Proceeds	Average Price Per 21 cwts.	Tons of Ore (21 cwts.)	Proceeds	Average Price 21 cwts.
		£	£-s-d		£	£-s-d
30.6.1815	92	646	7. 0. 5			
1816	786	3,966	5. 0.11			
1817	551	2,930	5. 6. 4			
1818	1,202	7,413	6. 3. 4			
1819	512	3,038	5.18. 8			
1820	321	1,428	4. 9. 0			
1821	766	6,335	8. 5. 5	331	2,489	7.10. 5
1822	2,844	18,263	6. 8. 5	2,399	16,793	7. 0. 0
TOTAL	7,074	44,019				
FOWEY CONSOLS						
1823	1,921	10,458	5. 8.11	2,256	13,391	5.18. 9
1824	2,634	15,906	6. 0. 9	2,390	14,548	6. 1. 9
1825	1,617	10,294	6. 7. 4	3,462	24,366	7. 0. 9
1826	2,471	14,934	6. 0.10	4,359	27,148	6. 4. 7
1827	3,226	16,432	5. 1.10	5,201	28,236	5. 8. 7
1828	4,216	23,494	5.11. 5	7,500	41,248	5.10. 0
1829	4,859	24,773	5. 2. 0	7,864	41,499	5. 5. 6
1830	7,085	36,696	5. 3. 7	6,152	32,648	5. 6. 2
1831	8,345	43,312	5. 3.10	4,554	24,828	5. 9. 0
1832	8,099	43,755	5. 8. 0	3,684	22,090	5.19.11
1833	9,292	51,879	5.11. 8	4,081	22,259	5. 9. 1
1.7.1833–31.12.1833	4,745	27,576	5.16. 3	2,206	12,249	5.11. 1
Calendar Year						
1834	9,667	58,240	6. 0. 6	3,739	18,185	4.17. 3
1835	11,010	66,964	6. 1. 8	2,373	11,189	4.16. 6
1836	14,007	97,997	6.19.11	425	2,207	5. 3.10
1837	15,711	89,084	5.13. 5			
1838	15,771	95,190	6. 0. 8	62,976	355,373	TOTAL
1.1.1839–30.6.1839	7,238	41,296	5.14. 1			

Year Ended	Tons of Ore (21 cwts.)	Proceeds £	Average Price Per 21 cwts £-s-d

FOWEY CONSOLS

Year Ended	Tons of Ore (21 cwts.)	Proceeds £	Average Price Per 21 cwts £-s-d
30.6.1840	12,560	68,662	5. 9. 4
1841	12,787	78,743	6. 3. 2
1842	13,289	78,467	5.18. 1
1843	12,755	72,700	5.14. 0
1844	12,341	66,591	5. 7.11
1845	9,809	49,730	5. 1. 5
1846	8,421	45,586	5. 8. 3
1847	6,105	32,127	5. 5. 3
1848	6,610	37,265	5.12. 9
1849	6,180	34,026	5.10. 1
1850	6,081	37,408	6. 3. 0
1851	5,831	33,332	5.14. 4
1852	4,756	27,215	5.14. 5
1853	4,294	32,066	7. 9. 4
1854	4,291	32,900	7.13. 4
1855	4,548	34,070	7. 9.10
1856	5,898	43,078	7. 6. 1
1857	5,817	42,967	7. 7. 9
1858	4,541	29,692	6.10. 9
1859	5,286	35,894	6.15.10
1860	4,821	33,733	6.19.11
1861	4,914	31,025	6. 6. 3
1862	4,456	26,332	5.18. 2
1863	3,943	20,864	5. 5.10
1864	3,600	20,791	5.15. 6
1865	3,247	15,659	4.16. 5
1866	2,705	13,083	4.16. 8
1867	1,333	5,040	3.15. 7
1868	176	760	4. 6. 4
TOTAL	313,309	1,848,086	

SUMMARY OF COPPER ORE PRODUCTION

	Year ended 30/6	Tons of Ore (21 cwts.)	Proceeds £
Wheal Treasure	1815–1822	7,074	44,019
Fowey Consols	1823–1868	313,309	1,848,086
Lanescot	1821–1836	62,976	355,373
TOTAL		383,359	2,247,478

Instead of the usual measurement of 20 cwts. to the ton it was the custom to take 21 cwts. to the mining 'ton' where copper ores were concerned. This was to save the smelting companies in South Wales from any possible loss in weight during the transport of the ores from Cornwall.

Very few of the original mine records from Fowey Consols exist, and the ore production figures have nearly all been obtained from secondary sources. The output from 1815 to 1832 is quoted in the various volumes of the Transactions of the Royal Geological Society of Cornwall. From the 1840s onwards annual production figures were quoted in the newspapers or in the Mining Journal. These were published using a twelve month period ending on the 30th June each year. To enable the mine's own figures to be used from the 1838 Report it has been necessary to quote six months output in 1833 and 1839 to fit in with the calendar year output quoted by the mine. The figures for Lanescot have been similarly adjusted. For the production figures not readily available local newspapers were examined and the output extracted from the weekly ticketing figures.

How accurate are they? The West Briton of 1.4.1842 quoted Treffry's own figures for the output of all the mines from August 1815 to the end of 1841 as follows: 234,486 tons and proceeds £1,422,633. This compares with figures extracted from independent sources as above giving 234,435 tons of copper ore, proceeds £1,360,134. There is a discrepancy of £62,499, which is 5% over the period in question. The difference is probably due to the mine adding transport costs on to the sale proceeds in its own books, as shown in the mine account for 1838 on page 69.

The Memoirs of the Geological Survey (Bodmin and St Austell) give a total output of 382,913 tons of copper ore for Fowey Consols and Lanescot, and this would appear to include the ore mined at Wheal Treasure. The recorded production of the three mines puts them third in the list of major copper mines in the south west of England.

Mine	Location	Copper Ore (21 cwts.)	Period
Devon Great Consols	Tavistock	742,400	1845–1903
Consolidated Mines	Gwennap	442,391	1815–1857
Fowey Consols & Lanescot	Tywardreath	383,359	1815–1867
United Mines	Gwennap	347,640	1815–1861

It is probable that the output from the two Gwennap mines above far exceeded the quoted figures. Gwennap Consols had worked on a very large scale in the second half of the eighteenth century, and in his book 'A History of Copper Mining in Cornwall and Devon' D. B. Barton estimates that their total production was approximately one million tons.

Figures for the other copper mines around St. Blazey are as follows:

	Copper Ore (21 cwts.)	
Par Consols	122,689	1841–1869
East Crinnis	86,070	1820–1841
Pembroke	85,900	1815–1867
Crinnis	67,429	1811–1833

APPENDIX II

DIVIDENDS & CALLS – FOWEY CONSOLS AND LANESCOT – CALENDAR YEARS

DIVIDENDS

		£
PRIOR TO 1834		83,286
1834		7,424
1835		10,240
1836	512 shares issued on consolidation with Lanescot	12,672
1837		14,208
1838		17,408
1839		18,432
1840 1841		10,243
1842		6,400
1843		9,728
1844 1845		12,603
1846–1849	1848 – shares reduced to 494	NIL
1850		1,976
1851–1854		NIL
1855		988
1856	shares sub-divided into 4940	3,705
1857		1,482
1858–1859		NIL
1860		1,235
1861		NIL
1862		700
1863–1864		NIL
		212,730

CALLS

		£	
1865	14/6 per share	3,581	These figures assume all the calls
1866	10/- per share	2,470	were fully paid. This is unlikely.
1867	3/- per share	741	
		6,792	

DIVIDENDS

1868
1869   See notes over.

Notes on dividends and calls

The dividend figures to 1838 are taken from the 1838 Report. The 1839 figure is taken from a letter written by J. T. Treffry in 1840 (TF932 at the CRO) and dividends totalling £10,243 must have been paid in 1840 and 1841 to bring them to a total dividend for the mines of £173,913 to the end of 1841 (WB 1.4.1842). The 1842 and 1843 dividends are taken from the MJ of 25.5.1844 with dividends calculated at £12,603 for 1844 and 1845 to agree with the figures shown in the MJ of 8.4.1854 covering the period 1846–1853 inc. and prior years. Subsequently dividends and calls are taken from X55–17 at the CRO and newspaper reports.

Incomplete records have been seen for 1868 and 1869 when dividends were paid from money received on the sale of the machinery and equipment. 4,527 shares were still in issue (the Treffry Estate owned 3,930) and dividends known to have been paid from the sale proceeds are 4/- per share in February 1868 and 2/- per share in November 1869.

APPENDIX III

FINAL SALE OF MINE MACHINERY AND EQUIPMENT

The following advertisement appeared in the Royal Cornwall Gazette of 4th July 1867:-

FOR SALE BY PUBLIC AUCTION

On Monday, July 15th, 1867, at Ten o'clock in the Forenoon, at FOWEY CONSOLS MINE, Tywardreath, near Par Station, the undermentioned valuable

MINE MACHINERY AND MATERIALS, Viz:-

80-in Cylinder ENGINE, 10ft 3-in. by 9ft 3-in. stroke, with 4 boilers, 12 tons each, and fittings
Two 22-in. Winding Engines, 5ft stroke, boilers and cages complete.
One 18-in.   do   4ft   do   do   do
Two 22-in. hydraulic engines.
11 water wheels of various sizes, from 16 to 40 ft diameter.
Rods, bobs and working gear for man engine.
2 drawing machines, worked by water wheels.
1 saw mill,   do   do
1 copper ore crusher   do   do
Patent separators   do   do
2 water stamps with iron axles, together 56 heads.
A large quantity of Memel and red pine main rods, varying from 6 to 14 inches, with hammered iron plates and rod pins to match.
Upwards of 400 pumps, various sizes, from 7 to 17 inches diameter.
A quantity of flange and door pins, pump rings, etc. etc.
14 H pieces, from 8 to 18-inch diameter.
20 door pieces, from 8 to 18-inch diameter.

14 plunger poles, from 6 to 15 inch diameter, with stuffing boxes, Glands, and Brass Bushings.

16 flat bottom and sinking windbores of different sizes.

A large quantity of bucket prongs, and brasses.

Do   do iron stave ladders.

Do   do staples and glands.

Do   do flat rope and other shieves, from 2 to 9 ft. diameter.

Crab winches of different sizes.

Hand and side screws of   do.

5 capstans and shears of   do.

15 balance bobs with castings, brasses etc.

450 fms. 12 in. shroud laid capstan ropes, 100 fms. of which is new.

5 and 7 in. flat ropes, horse whim ropes.

Upwards of 100 tons railroad iron.

Several tons railroad saddles.

Several tram waggons.

Several horse whims.

A large quantity of good useful timber.

Do   of new and old iron.

Do   Smith's bellows and tools, miners tools, Barrows etc.

A superior large turret clock, complete, with two dials.

And a variety of other articles and effects in general use in a large mine.

The whole will be offered in one lot, and if not disposed of, then to be sold separately.

The above may be inspected on application to the Agents on the mine, or further particulars obtained from Wm. WEST, Esq., Treden- ham House, St. Blazey, Mr Wm. POLKINGHORNE, Woodlands, Par Station, Cap. FRANCIS PUCKEY, St. Blazey, or

Mr. WILLIAM WERRY,

Dated June 20th, 1867.   Auctioneer, St. Blazey.

APPENDIX IV

MINERALS REPORTED AT FOWEY CONSOLS AND LANESCOT

Chalcopyrite is the main commercial source of copper. The principal copper ores mined at Fowey Consols and Lanescot were probably the following:-

Sometimes known as	Mineral	% of copper in pure specimens
Yellow copper ore	Chalcopyrite	34.5%
Grey copper ore	Chalcocite	79.8%
Red copper ore	Cuprite	88.8%
Black copper ore	Tenorite	79.8%

In practice absolutely pure specimens are rarely found and overall the Fowey Consols ores produced 7.8% copper and Lanescot 8.1%.

I am most grateful to Courtenay V. Smale for providing me with the following list of notable minerals found at the mines:-

NATIVE ELEMENTS
Silver
Copper

SULPHIDES
*Bismuthinite	Bismuth trisulphide.
Chalcocite	Cuprous sulphide.
Chalcopyrite	Sulphide of copper and iron.
Cobaltite	Sulpharsenide of cobalt and iron.
Marcasite	Disulphide of iron.
Millerite	Nickel sulphide.
Niccolite	Nickel arsenide.
Pyrite	Disulphide of iron.
Skutterudite	Cobalt and nickel arsenide.
Sphalerite	Zinc sulphide.
Stannite	Sulphide of copper, iron and tin.
Stibnite	Antimony trisulphide.

OXIDES
Cassiterite	Tin dioxide.

*Cuprite	(var. Chalcotrichite) Cuprous oxide.
Tenorite	Oxide of copper.
Magnetite	Oxide of iron.

CARBONATES

Malachite	Basic carbonate of copper.
Siderite	Ferrous carbonate.
Smithsonite	Carbonate of zinc.

SULPHATES

Brochantite	Basic sulphate of copper.
Devilline	Hydrated basic sulphate of copper and calcium.
Langite	Hydrated basic sulphate of copper.
Melanterite	Ferrous sulphate heptahydrate.
Posnjakite	Hydrated basic sulphate of copper.

PHOSPHATES

*Fluorapatite	(var. Francolite) Carbonatian fluo-phosphate of calcium.
*Rhabdophane	Hydrated phosphate of cerium, yttrium and other rare earth elements.
Torbernite	Hydrated phosphate of copper and uranium.

ARSENATES

| Annabergite | Hydrated arsenate of cobalt and nickel. |

SILICATES

| Actinolite | Basic silicate of calcium, magnesium and iron. |
| Hemimorphite | Basic hydrated silicate of zinc. |

*Museum quality specimens of these minerals have been found at Fowey Consols. Bismuthinite in long prismatic grey metallic crystals often associated with chalcopyrite probably originated from the Crosspark lode or Williams's lode. Chalcotrichite in brilliant-lustre red capillary crystals are amongst the finest ever found in Cornwall. Rhabdophane, one of the rarest minerals recorded from Cornwall, collected by Arthur Kingsbury of Oxford University in 1943 from the dumps at the mine, confirmed Fowey Consols as the first in Cornwall of which the location is certain. The mineral occurs in botryoidal or globular form, having a waxy lustre and clove-brown colour.

APPENDIX V

NOTES ON STEAM ENGINES AND WATER PRESSURE ENGINES

Prior to the 1830s it is not possible to give an accurate history of the engines on the mine. The water pressure engines were probably installed after 21st June 1825 when Thomas Petherick wrote to J. T. Austen: "I can by no means advise the disposal of any part of our machinery – even if we adopt pressure engines." John Farey found five of these engines at work in 1831, and there were only two remaining at the time of the 1838 mine report. The table below lists known engines and their shafts:-

Austen's	Bottrall's	Hodge's
80" pumping 1834–1867	22" whim (Davis's) 1837–1867	24" whim 1843–1855
	24" water pressure engine – later replaced by a 22" water pressure engine after 1844. 1829 (?)–1867	18" water pressure engine installed after 1838. 1843 (?) – 1855 (?).

Powne's	Ray's	Sawle's
18" whim* 1832 (?)–1838 22" whim 1838–1867	21" pumping ?–1832 18" whim 1832 – 1867	24" pumping 1832–1838.

Trathan's	Union	Henrietta's
20″ whim 1832–1860 (Reconstructed from an old steam whim on the mine prior to 1832, and moved to Kendall's North shaft in 1860).	40″ pumping 1826–1834. 22(½)″ water pressure engine installed prior to 1831–1867.	80″ pumping 1840–1843.
Kendall's North 20″ whim 1860–1862 (sold along with the north eastern part of the sett in 1862).	*This whim was positioned to the north of Union shaft and could also wind out of Union shaft.	

There appears to be little doubt that Austen's engine shaft and adjacent whim shaft were positioned in anticipation of a major expansion to the north. A copy of a letter dated 28th April 1834, probably sent to Thomas Robins by Austen, states: "as our great engine at Fowey Consols mine will go to work on Saturday I should wish on the spot to point out to you how much better we could, by the power that engine will afford us, work Mr Rashleigh's Carruggatt estate in search of minerals than any other – in fact no other company can work it efficiently." Six days later the famous 80″ engine started work, but it was destined to remain on the fringes of the underground workings. When Fowey Consols closed the engine was pumping from the 180 fathom level or thereabouts. The 22(½)″ water pressure engine at Union shaft was pumping from the 250 fathom level and all the deep eastern section of the mine appears to have been kept dry by the 22″ water pressure engine at Bottrall's shaft pumping from the 300 fathom level. This latter shaft was approximately 600 yards away from the steam engine at Austen's shaft, and this would appear to indicate that either Fowey Consols was a relatively dry mine or that the water pressure engines were very effective. Their operation would have been helped by the additional water coming on to the mine following the completion of the Luxulyan viaduct in 1842, and this may have played a part in the decision to move the 80″ engine at Henrietta's shaft to Par Consols in the period 1843/44. Dwindling hopes of success to the north of Austen's shaft continued almost to the closure of Fowey Consols, and despite the years of disappointment the lure of Carruggatt and Polharmon was still evident in a letter to the Mining Journal of 19th February 1881 and signed 'A Miner'. He considered that this area was still worth further investigation, and he wrote: "hearing that Capt. P. Rich had cut some good ore there, I was much pained to find that he was not supported by the retention of Austen's engine, where it stood to keep him dry, and enable an effectual development." At the time Philip Rich was the mineral agent for several landowners in the area, having been an agent at Fowey Consols from 1850 until it closed.

If Austen's engine was comparatively lightly used then the same could not be said for the 80″ engine transferred from Henrietta's shaft to Treffry's North shaft at Par Consols. The Mining Journal of 17th November 1860 quoted part of a Par Consols report commenting on the installation of a new 70″ engine on Meredith's shaft there "which will be a great relief to Treffry's North over taxed pumping engine." As well as these two engines in the eastern part of the mine, in the western section there was another 80" engine on Puckey's North shaft and a 72″ Bull engine on Puckey's shaft. Bull engines were a departure from the usual Cornish pumping engine. The beam was dispensed with, the cylinder was inverted directly over the shaft and the pump rod was connected directly to the piston rod.

This arrangement was also common in many water pressure engines where the weight of water in a vertical pipe, the pressure column, pushed up the piston in the cylinder which raised the main pump rod. Richard Trevithick was one of the engineers who developed this type of pump at the end of the eighteenth century. In its final form a system of valves was employed to control the entry and exit of water to and from the cylinder, creating a continuous pumping cycle. Ken Brown has kindly provided the following diagrams and description of the working cycle of a typical single acting engine:-

The Water Pressure Engine

A water pressure engine used the weight of water in a vertical pipe, the pressure column, to push up a piston in a cylinder which raised pump rods which were attached to one or more plunger pumps in a shaft. Richard Trevithick was the engineer credited with developing this type of pump at the end of the eighteenth century. In its final form a system of valves was employed to control the entry and exit of water to and from the cylinder creating a continuous pumping cycle.

Fig. 1 The Upward Stroke

With the engine at rest, the main piston P in the cylinder B and the pump rod R in the shaft, to which it is connected by piston rod N, are in the down position. To start the engine, water from the pressure column C is admitted to the bottom of the cylinder via the entry pipe A, the space between the piston valves P1 and P2 and via the port E. The water pressure causes the piston P to rise, thus raising the pump rod. Any water and air in the space above P is expelled through vent V. To allow the flow to take place, the piston assembly P1, P2 is held down by water pressure acting on top of P1. This is derived from the pressure column C via the shuttle cylinder G and pipes K and H. The space between P1 and P2 is also in constant communication with the water in the pressure column via the pipe A but to hold P1 and P2 down, the former is of slightly larger diameter.

The position of P1 and P2 is in turn controlled by the 'shuttle' valve assembly F1 and F2 which works in a shuttle cylinder G and is connected to a control rod D. The space between F1 and F2 is also in constant communication with the pressure column via the small bore pipe H. The valve chest L is of two diameters, to match the slightly larger diameter of piston valve P1. To hold the piston valves in the down position, shuttle piston F1 is raised by the down position of the pump rod to which it is connected via the linkage R, J and T.

As the pump rod R rises, so the linkage J and slotted link M also rise until the bottom of the slot in M engages the pin on the arm of the tumbling counterweight T making it tip the other way. This brings down the control rod D and shuttle pistons F1 and F2. (An alternative way of operating the tumbling counterweight was by means of tappets).

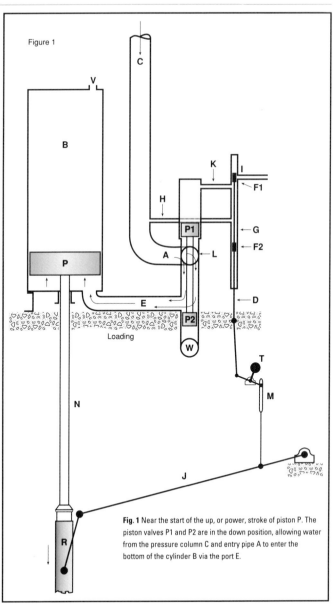

Figure 1

Loading

Fig. 1 Near the start of the up, or power, stroke of piston P. The piston valves P1 and P2 are in the down position, allowing water from the pressure column C and entry pipe A to enter the bottom of the cylinder B via the port E.

A piston valve example of a water pressure engine is shown diagrammatically in Figs 1 and 2. Certain features such as the sluice valves, regulating cocks and joint flanges are omitted for clarity. (The source material for the diagrams is *Records of Mining and Metallurgy* by Phillips and Darlington, published in 1857)

Fig. 2 The Downward Stroke

Lowering shuttle pistons F1 and F2 causes the former to blank off the pipe K and uncover the exhaust vent I. This releases the pressure acting above piston valve P1, allowing both valves to rise to the new position shown, due to the pressure between them and the larger diameter of P1. P2 has now cut off the flow of water from the pressure column and, by uncovering the port E, allows the water below the main piston P to escape through E and the exhaust pipe W.

The pump rod in the shaft now descends under its own weight, causing the plungers attached to it in the shaft to force mine water from underground up the rising main. (These pumping arrangements are conventional and are not shown). When the main piston P approaches the end of its travel, the linkage J and the slotted linkage M tip the tumbling counterweight back to its original position, raising the small pistons F1 and F2 and causes the cycle to repeat. The engine will continue at work until the supply of water from the pressure column is cut off.

As with steam engines the size of water pressure engines was given by the diameter of the cylinder in which the main piston operated expressed in inches.

The water pressure engine's at Fowey Consols were installed well below the shaft collar to obtain the necessary height for the column of water in the pressure column C. The water exhaust from the engines was discharged with the mine water through the adit.

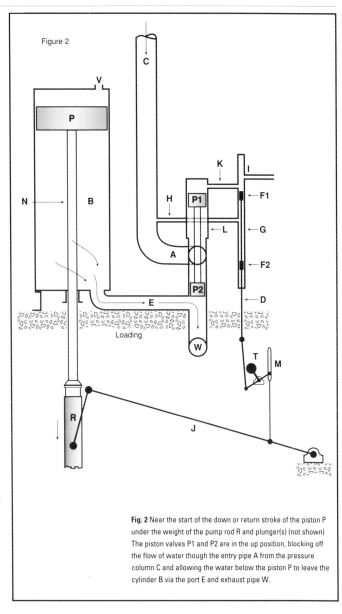

Figure 2

Loading

Fig. 2 Near the start of the down or return stroke of the piston P under the weight of the pump rod R and plunger(s) (not shown) The piston valves P1 and P2 are in the up position, blocking off the flow of water though the entry pipe A from the pressure column C and allowing the water below the piston P to leave the cylinder B via the port E and exhaust pipe W.

APPENDIX VI

A DESCRIPTION OF THE CHANGING AND DRYING HOUSES AT FOWEY CONSOLS TAKEN FROM THE PARLIAMENTARY COMMISSION REPORT OF 1864

"In the eastern part[1] there is one changing house, a dry, and two runs of barracks. The change is a stone building 42 feet long, 16 feet wide, and 7 feet high, with a spring roof of 6 feet, making a clear height in the centre of 13 feet. The roof is a good slate one, plastered inside. There are two openings on each about 2½ feet square, furnished with shutters; and also a doorway 5½ x 3 feet, but no door. There is no roof ventilation. The floor, I imagine, is a stone or earthen one, but there are several inches of dirt and accumulated rubbish upon it so that it cannot be seen. The roof and all parts of the woodwork are covered thickly with accumulated dirt. There is no provision made for the men to wash themselves, any more than a stream of water running along outside. About 30 men use this house. The men stand upon their hutches[2] while changing.

The dry is about 30 feet long by 12 feet wide. It is warmed by means of a fire, the smoke and heat of which pass through a series of three pipes before entering the stack. The men's clothes are dried on these pipes. The shutters of the windows are studiously kept closed to prevent loss of heat, there is no roof ventilation, therefore the house is most offensively close, and the clothes instead of being sweetened to some extent by a circulation of warm, dry fresh air, are simply dried, and retain all the offensive matter given off by the men while at work. This is a point of some considerable importance, as I am told that the men rarely, if ever, wash their flannels. A man is kept to look after the dry.

The sump men and pitmen have each a changing and drying house to themselves.

The floor is covered to some thickness with dirt so that there is a continued stirring up of dust every time a number of men enter the house, which of course falls upon and is retained by the wet clothes of the miners.

The changing house in the tutwork part of the mines[3] is of very good size, being 55 feet long, 24 feet wide, and 17 feet high. It is provided with six windows and a large doorway. The floor, as in other cases, is dirty in the extreme, and the walls and ledges covered with dirt. The men change standing on their hutches.[2] There is no fire, nor a supply of water.

The dry is 54 feet long by 15 feet wide. This is much better than the eastern dry, having a better floor and a small ventilator in the roof. It is warmed by a fire and pipes. It has also a large oven in which the men can warm their dinners, &c.

The men generally change here in the winter.

The barracks are merely long runs of low sheds, of stone and slate roofs, built for changes when the mine employed larger numbers of men. They are devoted now to the men for store houses.

The greater number of the females employed on the surface work in the open air. There are some sheds, but as they are only provided with roofs, without any sides, there is such a strong draught of air through, that the girls prefer being out of them. In case of wet weather, inasmuch as the mine is not working very extensively, the females stop work, they being able to dress all the ore in fine weather. There is a good house in the eastern part, of same size as the changing house, which is used for dressing purposes in wet weather.

During the summer the females eat their dinners etc. sitting about where they can, there being no place appropriated for them; in the winter a house is provided for them."

1. Near Bottrall's shaft.
2. Small chests.
3. Possibly the 'Tutworkmen's Barracks' shown on the de la Beche map.

INDEX